hotels • restaurants • shops • spas

balichic

GW00630819

hotels • restaurants • shops • spas

balichic

text susi johnston • don bosco

·K·U·P·E·R·A·R·D·

managing editor
melisa teo

editor
laura jeanne gobal

designer
annie teo

production manager
sin kam cheong

first published in 2004 by
editions didier millet pte ltd
121 telok ayer street, #03-01
singapore 068590
telephone : +65 6324 9260
facsimile : +65 6324 9261
email   : edm@edmbooks.com.sg
website   : www.edmbooks.com

first published in great britain 2005 by
kuperard
59 hutton grove, london n12 8ds
telephone : +44 (0) 20 8446 2440
facsimile : +44 (0) 20 8446 2441
enquiries : sales@kuperard.co.uk
website   : www.kuperard.co.uk

Kuperard is an imprint of Bravo Ltd.

©2004 editions didier millet pte ltd

Printed in Singapore

All rights reserved. No part of this publication may
be reproduced, stored in a retrieval system, or
transmitted in any form or by any means,
electronic, electrostatic, magnetic tape, mechanical,
photocopying, recording or otherwise, without prior
written permission from the publisher.

isbn: 1-85733-409-4

COVER CAPTIONS:
1: Treatment at Henna Spa
2: Spa details at Henna Spa
3: Poolside at Ibah Luxury Villas
4: Bali Museum
5: Cut rice for drying
6: Ducks in the rice fields
7: Mount Batur
8: Bali Aga villager
9: Bali's rice terraces
10: Stone carving
11: The surf in south Bali
12: Uma Ubud in central Bali
13: Sculpture at The Avatara
14: Stone sculpture at Uma Ubud
15: Alila Ubud's infinity-edged pool
16: Greenery at The Avatara
17: Doorway to a courtyard at Uma Ubud
18: Panelling at The Avatara
19: Floral details at Bagus Jati
20: Waka di Ume in central Bali
21: Waka Shorea in north Bali
22: Courtyard at Ibah Luxury Villas' spa
23: Pool at Bagus Jati

PAGE 2: Doorway at Villa Balquisse

THIS PAGE: Drinks at Puri Ganesha

OPPOSITE: Terrace at Villa Balquisse

PAGE 6: View of pool at Maya Ubud

PAGE 8 AND 9: Villa at Maya Ubud

contents

18 central+eastbali

108 south+westbali

200 northbali

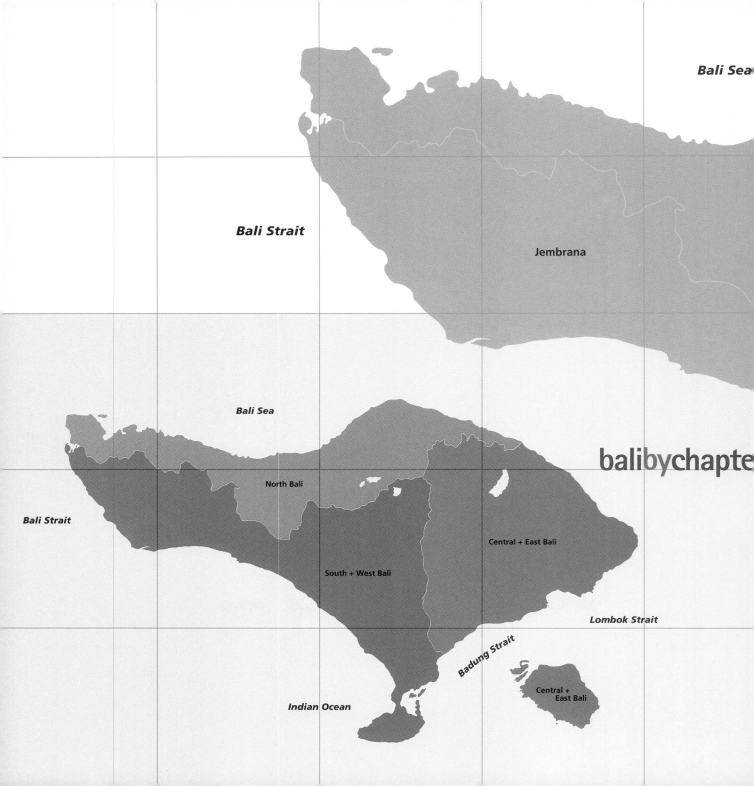

Bali Sea

Bali Strait

Jembrana

Bali Sea

North Bali

balibychapte

Central + East Bali

Bali Strait

South + West Bali

Lombok Strait

Badung Strait

Indian Ocean

Central +
East Bali

balibyregencies

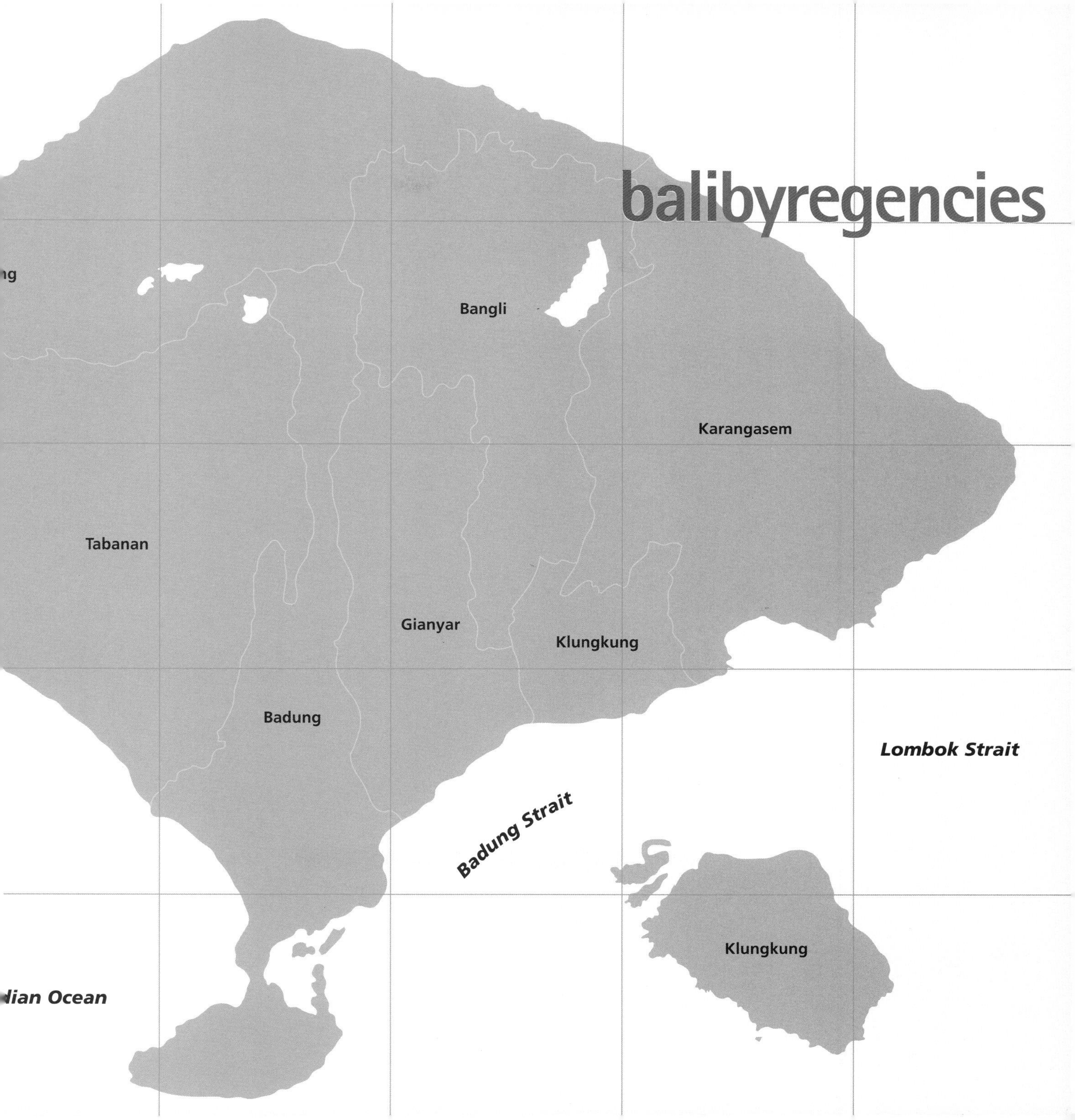

introduction

still vibrant and flourishing

Bali has certainly changed since tourism first made its debut here early in the 20th century. But the 'real Bali' still thrives, and like the scent of incense, cloves and flowers, it permeates every corner of the island and fills the atmosphere with something unforgettable. The unique culture of Bali is resilient, persistent and very much alive, not only in its small villages, but also in the towns and cities, where ancient traditions blend brilliantly with a burgeoning global lifestyle.

Rest assured that in spite of the pace of change, the 'real Bali' we all dream of—where sarong-clad beauties saunter with swaying hips towards ancient temples under twisted trees, bearing elegant offerings—still exists. So does the Bali where farmers in palm-leaf topees labour with unstudied grace in green rice fields alongside calmly snorting water buffalo and hurrying lines of little ducks.

Yes, the Bali that has always inspired such florid prose is still vibrant and flourishing, although it is now enhanced by sophisticated hotels, villas and restaurants, and the international ideas, ideals, lifestyles and facilities that go along with them.

Nevertheless, you will still be awestruck by vistas of smoking volcanoes silhouetted against the morning sky, thrilled by the clamour of clashing gongs, dazzled by the wild costumes of dancers glittering with gilded trim, and you will still find peaceful stretches of beach to loll on, thriving coral reefs to glide above, and lush rice fields to walk through.

the lie of the land

How can an island this small offer so much and allow such diversity to co-exist harmoniously? A lot of it has to do with the lie of the land and the landscape of Bali.

Bali is tall in the middle, with its highest point reaching over 3,000 m (9,842 ft). It has a line of volcanic mountains stretching across from east to west, some of which are covered with extremely thick vegetation that provides habitats for a variety of birds and wildlife, and they offer many opportunities for adventurous treks. Others, like Mount Batur, and the tallest of all, Mount Agung, offer wild moonscapes of volcanic

THIS PAGE (FROM TOP): In Bali, nature, society and spiritual life co-exist in a unique way; domesticated ducks make their way through the rice fields.
OPPOSITE: A quintessential Bali sunset, with Tanah Lot temple in the foreground.

rock and rubble. These dramatic, eerie, exposed and otherworldly scenes add to the mystical charm of the island.

The sides of these volcanoes slope dramatically downwards to the sea. Much of this terrain is covered with sculpted rice terraces or hectares of bamboo and primaeval forests. Elsewhere are clove, coffee and coconut plantations, along with orchards that provide livelihoods for the locals and shady cover for visitors embarking on country walks.

The sloping sides of Bali are sliced from peak to shore by steep river gorges which create stunning views and effective barriers to travel. Particularly in the mid to upper elevations, roads and paths meander along the ridges between the river gorges.

The mountainous centre of Bali affects its weather, making the north and south of the island quite different in terms of climate. The southern slopes are wet and green, and slope rather gently downwards to the sea. They enjoy generous rainfall, especially during the wet season from November to April. January and February can be utterly awash with rain, while June to September are often almost entirely rain free (except in the upper elevations). The northern slopes are drier and often hotter, with rainfall a rare occurrence even during the wet season. Consequently, the vegetation, agriculture and landscape varies from north to south.

marine and beach bali

Bali floats near the equator amid relatively cool, deep seas. This means the marine life offshore is lavishly diverse and the climate is tempered by the presence of so much water. There's spectacular diving at almost every compass point around the island.

Swimming, snorkelling and surfing can be enjoyed in quite shark-free waters. The only sharks you might see near the shore are small reef sharks which are not a threat to surfers, swimmers or snorkellers. Aggressive marine life, such as jellyfish which can make beach sojourns a pain, seem relatively rare here as well.

THIS PAGE: Salt panning and fishing in traditional outriggers provide a simple livelihood for communities along Bali's coasts.

OPPOSITE (FROM TOP): Whether you're in a fine dining restaurant or on the beach, you can expect excellent service.

Beaches in Bali can be wide and suitable for long walks, with sand in a pleasant beige hue, while others are gravel-like, or covered in grainy black sand that holds the heat like a brick oven. There are also a few powdery white-sand beaches, most notably just offshore on Nusa Lembongan, an outpost suited to water sports fanatics.

living large is easy living

One of the best things about Bali is the service. Here, you can truly 'live large', or be waited on hand and foot by genuinely friendly staff. This level of service is not about grovelling, it's about the true spirit of hospitality. Often, your wishes seem to have been anticipated and fulfilled before you even recognise them yourself.

Bali is also about living at ease. There is less struggle and confusion here than in other Asian vacation spots. It is more relaxed and offers an informal kind of comfort. The culture and social life of the island are as accessible as its sights. And it still offers a high level of safety and security with very low crime rates. This situation gives you the freedom to do as you please, without undue worry.

In Bali, the sophisticated and the primitive cohabit amicably. So you can live a life of adventure, and still sip a perfect cappucino or watch the BBC in the afternoon. You can easily rent a car or motorcycle and drive it yourself, or hire a car and driver and be guided through the island, at a reasonable price. Most roads are reliable, and all roads lead to somewhere interesting, so you're free to go, and keep going.

In Bali, you're always within one or two hours' drive of good food and very comfortable accommodation, and wherever you end up, you can get a bottle of pure drinking water, buy a snack, ask for directions or use a GSM mobile phone (buy one, or bring one and buy an affordable chip to put in it).

Practical things like credit cards, automatic teller machines, foreign exchange, international telephone lines, Internet connections and emergency services are all quite up to date and accessible. You can get away from it all, and stay connected at the same time. Now that's living large, with the best of both worlds.

THIS PAGE: *In the nurturing atmosphere of Bali, inner and outer worlds can find a delicate balance facilitated by meditation programmes at centres for well-being such as Bagus Jati.*

OPPOSITE: *Simplicity and luxury can meet in magical ways during a sojourn in Bali.*

living light

Bali runs much deeper than the material world of luxuries and fun. It is also a haven for those seeking to cultivate their inner being, or reinvigorate the youthful exuberance they sacrificed to the demands of modern life back home. This island paradise is not just a great place for extravagance, it is also a great place for simple living, natural healing and much-needed physical rejuvenation.

Bali has become a shining light in the world of mind, body and spiritual therapies, well-being retreats and beauty treatments. To revive your inner light, you can select from the many seminars, classes and workshops available throughout the island offering Reiki, Tai Chi, yoga, 'Light Language', martial arts, meditation, traditional medicine, Balinese mysticism, and other enlightening subjects.

And as far as spas are concerned, you'll be spoiled for choice. From small and friendly massage parlours and manicure salons, to ultra luxurious spas set in extensive grounds, it is all on offer, and at pleasingly competitive prices.

small island, infinite possibilities

Basically, Bali is just a small tropical island floating in the middle of Indonesia. In some ways it is like a small town—very approachable and intimate. In fact, a local expatriate pundit once quipped, "Stay in Bali for a year, and you'll know everyone on the island".

At the same time, Bali seems to offer limitless possibilities with something different to tempt even the most jaded traveller. Bali has become a crossroads of the world, where stars, styles and ideas from every culture meet and mix. Accordingly, the very same local expatriate pundit also said, "Stay in Bali for ten years, and you'll meet everyone in the world. Everyone worth meeting, that is".

For nearly a century, Bali has been drawing personalities from all four corners of the globe. People who can go anywhere they want to, go to Bali. And they often come back, time and again. That pundit of paradise may have been right: if you stay long enough, you just might meet them all.

People who can go anywhere they want to, go to Bali.

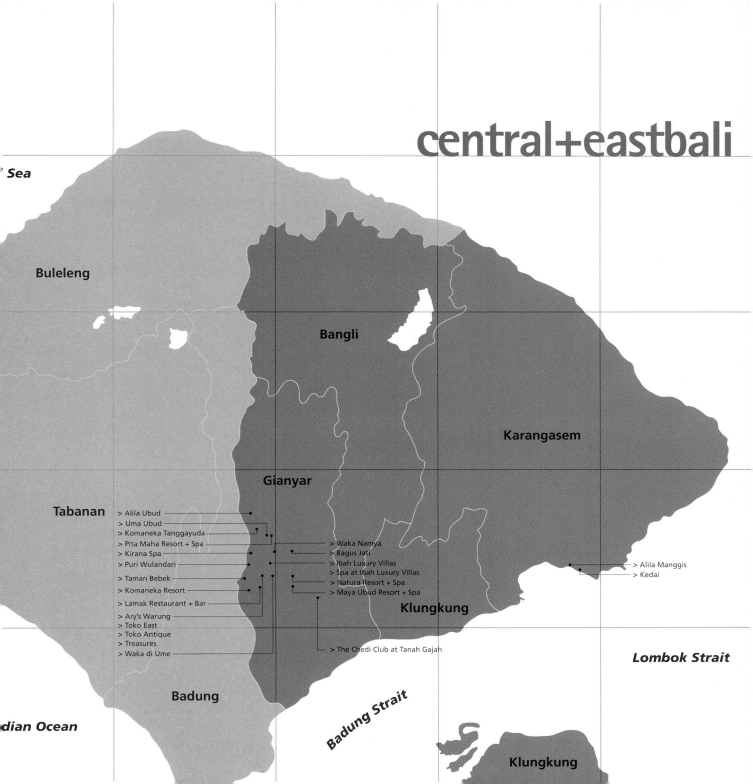

central+eastbali

Sea

Buleleng

Bangli

Karangasem

Gianyar

Tabanan

> Alila Ubud
> Uma Ubud
> Komaneka Tanggayuda
> Pita Maha Resort + Spa
> Kirana Spa
> Puri Wulandari
> Taman Bebek
> Komaneka Resort
> Lamak Restaurant + Bar

> Ary's Warung
> Toko East
> Toko Antique
> Treasures
> Waka di Ume

> Waka Namya
> Bagus Jati
> Ibah Luxury Villas
> Spa at Ibah Luxury Villas
> Natura Resort + Spa
> Maya Ubud Resort + Spa

Klungkung

> Alila Manggis
> Kedai

> The Chedi Club at Tanah Gajah

Lombok Strait

Badung

Badung Strait

dian Ocean

Klungkung

the heartland with a welcoming heart

Central and east Bali cover the entire upland interior of the island, as well as the towns and villages along the coastal areas of its eastern arm. It includes precipitous mountain passes and peaks, and innumerable sites of cultural and historical importance scattered over sloping terrain running downwards from the high volcanoes towards the more urban environs at Bali's southern tip. The middle elevations are almost totally covered with those famously green and fabulously sculpted rice terraces that Bali is known for.

This is the heartland of Bali, not only geographically, but also culturally, spiritually and historically. It is a region of great natural beauty, with dramatic mountain scenery and an equally dramatic cultural panorama. The performing and plastic arts here are nothing short of legendary, and are matched in stature by the area's lively ritual life, architecture, antiquities and traditional crafts. The people of Bali's heartland are, as a rule, genuinely eager to get to know foreign visitors. Any traveller who shows a modicum of interest and respect is likely to find themselves welcomed eagerly into the daily world of the Balinese, whether that world is a simple farming village or a splendid royal palace encrusted with elaborate gilt carvings.

In the midst of all this lies the most popular destination in central Bali, Ubud. Once a sleepy artists' village, it is now a mini-metropolis ringed by some of the most luxurious and innovative resort properties in Asia. Outside of the Ubud area, almost all of central and east Bali remains distinctly Balinese, with traditional culture that is largely intact because it is not driven by tourism or focused primarily on tourists.

a postcard you can walk right into

The sights and sounds we associate with 'the real Bali' can all be found here, where the Bali of postcards and glossy books comes alive before your eyes, even today, in the 21st century. Only now, the ancient traditions and lush tropical scenery are complemented by facilities and services to spoil even the most demanding traveller. It is fair to say that the heartlands and uplands of Bali combine the best of both worlds.

PAGE 18: *Even agriculture in Bali is artistic, as evidenced by the undulating rice terraces.*

THIS PAGE (FROM TOP): *Dugout canoes are still used by villagers along the shores of Lake Tamblingan; rice terraces are studded with little shelters called kubu where farmers can take a break.*

OPPOSITE: *Although it appears serene, Mount Batur is an active volcano, occasionally rumbling with activity.*

To experience the Bali of postcards, base yourself in Ubud or the seaside town of Manggis, and embark on day trips to explore as far afield as you like. Although the area is vast, the distances between places are not great, leaving the whole region within easy reach of a base around these towns.

history is a feeling

In the villages and countryside of central and east Bali, the presence of history is palpable. From the Bronze Age to the 20th century, central and east Bali set the stage for a historical story that reads like a fairy tale, full of competing kingdoms, power struggles, pitched battles, wandering mystics and powerful priests. These days, all of central and east Bali is a historical and archaeological treasure trove.

In addition to the many ancient sites listed in guidebooks, almost every town and village has its own legends, artefacts and sacred sites linking it to the distant past. Just ask the locals, explore on your own by car or on foot, and browse the guidebooks to find clues to the mysteries of Bali's past. To best appreciate the layers of history that shape this region, enlist the help of a driver-guide and set off for the day to visit temples, palaces and sacred springs. Don't get stuck on an itinerary, however, follow your instincts, take an inviting side road, stop the car and investigate all the places that call out to you or look like they might offer some interesting sights.

In Bali's countryside, visitors are generally very welcome to get out of the car and walk into the postcard, so to speak. There aren't laws against trespassing per se, although one should always respect the property and privacy of others. Furthermore, when you approach a temple, you are required to don a sarong and sash before entering its gates, even when the temples are empty and silent, so always carry these essential items with you on day trips.

THIS PAGE (FROM TOP): *Besakih is a complex of temples punctuated by towering meru shrines thatched with black palm fibre; a stone sculpture expresses the deep reverence which the Balinese have for their deities, ancestors and the natural world.*

OPPOSITE: *Shrines and offerings, particularly directed at Dewi Sri, the goddess of rice and fertility, are everywhere; temples consist of walled courtyards filled with shrines and pavilions open to the sky.*

a rich tapestry of religious beliefs

Traditional culture is the reason many travellers visit central and east Bali, and the underlying fabric of all Balinese culture is its religion. Although referred to as Balinese Hinduism, it doesn't much resemble the Hinduism you may be familiar with. The Balinese version is a syncretic one, with many threads sewn into a rich tapestry.

The religion of Bali has its roots in the animistic beliefs of pre-historic times, with various superstitions and rituals related to ancestor worship, fertility and survival. Features of the landscape are treated as spiritually powerful and invisible forces are assumed to be at play in everything around us. On this foundation of mysticism and superstition, Balinese Hinduism is constructed in layers, having taken elements from many of the cultures and historical periods that influenced it during the past two millennia. Tantric Buddhism has left a strong impression, as have elements of Indian Hinduism, particularly of the Shiva-worshipping sects, and Chinese folk beliefs, with a little Indonesian-style Islam to spice up the mix.

The result is an incredibly complex set of beliefs and practices that shape almost every aspect of Balinese life. Every day, week, lunar month and solar year is measured out and given spiritual and folkloric significance, and every activity has its patron spirits, powers and practices. The Hindu caste system also survives in Bali, although in a somewhat modernised way, incorporating more flexibility than in previous times.

One needn't rush off to a large, publicised ritual event to enjoy the pageantry of Balinese religious life. There are offerings made and rituals carried out almost everywhere, every day and every hour. Some are very small, like the daily offerings which honour and placate the various powers. Other ceremonies are larger in scale and elaborately staged, lasting for weeks with mass processions, mountains of offerings and solemn rituals officiated by many high priests at once.

In central and east Bali, where tradition is still very much alive, one needn't go far to learn about and appreciate Balinese Hinduism and its rituals. Just take a walk or ask the locals you meet about ceremonies you might be allowed to attend.

peak experiences on bali's volcanoes

Exploration and opportunities for adventure abound in the mountains of central and east Bali, with six mountain areas of particular interest for the visitor. Moving from west to east, they are the Pupuan area, Mount Batukaru, Bedugul, Mount Batur and its neighbours, Mount Agung and Mount Lempuyang.

The Belimbing to Pupuan road has splendid views of rice terraces climbing up almost to the sky. At the top is a mountain pass which is one of several gateways to north Bali. Located along the route upwards to Pupuan are several eco- and agritourism programmes offering a detailed look into the world of highland farming. The plantations here harvest an array of tropical crops including vanilla, chocolate, coffee, cloves, starfruit and vegetables. Short hikes lead to scenic waterfalls and viewpoints. For specifics about routes, just ask a local guide or enquire at a local café or hotel.

THIS PAGE: *Bali's volcanoes dramatically illustrate the forces that have shaped the island, and their eruptions contribute to the fertility of its soil.*

OPPOSITE (FROM TOP): *The rustic elegance of Waka di Ume is inspired by the simple traditions of village life; climbing to the top of Mount Lempuyang in east Bali is a pleasant pilgrimage requiring no special equipment.*

Not far east of Pupuan is Mount Batukaru, a sacred peak with virgin forests teeming with wildlife. On the upper slopes of Batukaru is the temple of the same name, which is among the most sacred sites on the island. It has been renovated in recent years but a sense of peace and mystery still prevails amid its courtyards and ancient shrines. Its lake and holy water spring lend an air of magic to this sanctuary. The mountain villages and landscapes throughout the Batukaru area are laced together by side roads that invite exploration, but there's not much in the way of facilities for visitors. Adventurous travellers might enjoy a steep day trek or hike to the summit.

The next mountain area, moving eastward from Batukaru, is Bedugul, an extensive region with all manner of recreation. On the scenic end of the scale are the botanical gardens and the Bali Handara Kosaido Country Club, where you can play a round of golf in a lush, garden-like setting with a unique twist—the entire course is located inside a vast volcanic crater. There are three main lakes in Bedugul, two of which fall in the sublime category—Beratan and Tamblingan. Both are in pleasant, natural settings offering opportunities for walks, relaxation and exploration. They are less travelled and less obstructed than their larger counterpart, Lake Buyan.

The main tourist zone beside Lake Beratan is a favourite stop for local Indonesian tourists who can be a rambunctious and noisy bunch, particularly on Sundays and school holidays. The nearby temple, Pura Ulun Danu, provides one of the most memorable sights on the entire island, and one of the most photographed. The temple literally rises up out of the lake, with its tiered shrines reflected on the waters.

Moving eastward again, the next mountain region of interest is the Batur area, with Bali's most active volcano looming large and smouldering over a massive crater lake. Although the tourist facilities on the crater's rim are rather dire, that does not mean the area is spoiled by any means. The scenery is outstanding and if the volcano is in a lively mood, you may see smoke, fire and spitting stones. Despite the multitude of restaurants and cafés here, you won't be able to get yourself a decent meal for love or money, so come prepared. The wide, open landscape of volcanic debris down on the

crater floor, along the shores of the lake, is quite dramatic. A walk to the summit of Mount Batur at sunrise is one of the most popular trekking itineraries in Bali, and those who have done it, almost without exception give the excursion rave reviews. A local guide and good weather are musts for this little expedition.

The Batur area has some wonderful temples, notably Pura Ulun Danau Batur—often cited as the second most holy temple in Bali—located on the main road at the crater's rim. Smaller and more mysterious is the Pucak Penulisan temple, also known as Pura Tegeh Koripan, further north along the road at the town of Penulisan or Sukawana. To reach the temple, you will have to climb a few hundred steps, and at the top you will find an exceedingly ancient temple, shrouded in mystery. It houses a remarkable collection of religious statuary which dates back about 1,000 years, when a great kingdom based in this area held sway over the island.

Moving eastward again, one comes to the next mountain landmark for visitors, Mount Agung. The high road leading from the Batur crater town of Penelokan, past Batu Dinding and towards Rendang, is one of the most scenic drives in Bali, with roadside viewpoints along a knife-edge ridge above Batur's lake. Mount Agung is Bali's highest peak and the location of its top-ranking temple, Besakih, also known as 'the mother temple'. Besakih is a vast complex, but unfortunately is not managed well as a cultural and historical destination. For those who would feel they hadn't been to Bali without visiting its highest peak, yes, do go, but otherwise, perhaps your time would be better spent elsewhere on the mountain.

The open slopes and windswept landscapes of Mount Agung are better appreciated from one of the less-travelled roads that meander up its sides. There are several choices and every one of them leads to great views. Each 'non-Besakih' road has surprises in store for the curious—small, remote villages, unusual temples, strange plant and animal life, and wide, open spaces dropping steeply down to reveal all of Bali spread out at your feet. Summit treks on Agung are tough but rewarding and require a local guide. This can be arranged through hotel concierge desks.

Finally, at the far eastern end of Bali is one of the most charming and fascinating mountain areas of all, Mount Lempuyang, its near-perfect cone punctuating Bali's eastern edge. A temple crowns the mountain, built in tiers with a stunning white stone enclosure at its main level. This gives way to a well-maintained path with conveniently paved steps leading upwards to the sky, past each of the higher shrines of the Lempuyang complex, to the summit where a small temple with several shrines exudes a very strong sense of sacred power. The views this hike affords, overlooking east Bali and Mount Agung, are unsurpassed. At every step along the way, one feels compelled to turn around and look down at the sweeping panorama, and across to the volcanic cone of Mount Agung.

water, water everywhere

Water, in the form of rain, rivers, lakes and sea is elemental and essential to central Bali, its culture, agriculture and religion. Water temples, water palaces, dramatic rainstorms, springs, waterfalls and the sea all contribute considerably to the area's magic. Water is also responsible for one of the most quintessential features of its landscape—the sculpted rice terraces.

An unfathomably complex system of irrigation canals and aqueducts form a web of water over much of Bali's interior. This vast system dates back several thousand years or more to ancient hydraulic engineers who were the ancestors of today's Balinese. Wet rice farming, fostered by the careful distribution of water flowing down Bali's slopes, was the foundation of the island's rich culture, relative prosperity and robust population, and one of the reasons for its popularity with visitors. The fantastically built rice terraces and the marvellous views they afford are one of the most magical aspects

THIS PAGE: The Ulun Danu Beratan temple near Bedugul seems to float on the lake, and is one of the most photographed sights on the island.
OPPOSITE (FROM TOP): Bali Handara Kosaido Country Club is ensconced within the extinct crater of a volcano; temples in the mountains are cool and misty, many of them made from a hard, dark lava stone that is found at high elevations.

THIS PAGE: *Rice is still planted and harvested entirely by hand in Bali, with the cycle of planting and harvesting being an important element of village cohesion.*
OPPOSITE: *A walk in Ubud's countryside promises many surprises such as a scenic riverside or a whimsical scarecrow fashioned from the simplest of materials.*

of Bali. A traveller hasn't experienced the place until he has walked amid the rice terraces, particularly in the soft, golden light of late afternoon.

The rivers of central and east Bali tumble down from summit to shore in leafy gorges, making excellent runs for river rafting. Some of them drop out of sight into the geological 'swiss cheese' beneath the island's surface, flowing underground, then popping out of the cliffs and valley floors downslope in dramatic fashion. The resulting powerful ground springs and cliffside spouting springs dot the middle and high elevations. Many are considered holy, their pure waters set aside to sanctify offerings or to cleanse spiritual impurity. Others are gathering places for daily bathing and washing, alive with jollity and play, particularly in the late afternoon when parents, children and teenagers gather to clean up and catch up on the latest gossip.

an accessible arts scene

While Ubud is recognised as its artistic heart, the entire region of central and east Bali is filled with creativity. Art in all forms, from basketry, metalworking and lontar palm leaf inscribing, to comedic drama and clashing gamelan performances can be found almost everywhere in Bali's heartland. The arts are an integral part of life here, particularly of ritual life, so the whole place is like a non-stop festival of abundant artistic creation and lavish performances.

There are so many traditional dance and drama performances in the Ubud area alone that you might drive yourself to distraction just trying to decide which to see. But don't feel any pressure about it, because there will always be more tomorrow. In addition to daily performances at about a dozen venues in the area, there are constant temple ceremonies, with rituals, processions, dance, music and shadow puppet performances to entertain the community and honour their gods and ancestors. And don't scoff at the nightly dances organised for tourists either. They are superbly performed by some of the most talented artists in Bali, in fact, the same ones who dance at the grand temple ceremonies.

For painting and sculpture, Ubud is a good place to start, with a range of galleries on its main streets and in the neighbouring villages. They offer everything from works of merely decorative merit, right up to museum-quality masterpieces by established and internationally renowned artists. There has been an increasing interest in 20th-century and contemporary Indonesian painters, and many of them, whether born Balinese or not, have found themselves working in Bali during part or all of their careers, and selling their paintings here. So, whether you're a purveyor of fine art, or looking for something simple and distinctive to commemorate your visit to Bali, you should find it without too much effort in Ubud.

To get an idea of which painters you like and what the going prices are, buy an auction catalogue from Larasati, which is an art auction house based in Jakarta and Singapore. The catalogues are also available in the more modern bookshops of Ubud, the airport and other international shopping areas of Bali. Sotheby's and Christie's also periodically auction Indonesian paintings and works of art, so their catalogues are another enjoyable resource to educate your eye, as are the collections of the many art museums around Ubud. Do your homework, then peruse the major art galleries of Ubud, like Sumertha, Rudana, Komaneka, Agung Rai and Neka to view the works there from an informed standpoint.

THIS PAGE (FROM TOP): Local men rehearse the ancient baris warrior dance; shops in Ubud offer all sorts of knick-knacks; Ubud's main street is flanked by inviting cafés and shops to while away the hours. OPPOSITE: Woodcarvers in the towns surrounding Ubud are both prolific and inventive.

shopping is an art in itself

Travellers who don't care to launch into the upper reaches of art collecting will be extremely well served in the Ubud area and surrounding communities as well. There are works of art and handicrafts in a variety of media available, and in every price range. And there is no need to be intimidated here. If you like it, buy it. But remember that bargaining is an essential skill, particularly when buying art or handicrafts, where value can be subjective and open to interpretation.

Shopping is a fully legitimate pastime in its own right in central and east Bali. The range of handicrafts, accessories, gifts and furniture is so broad that it defies description. Better see for yourself and caveat emptor. Prices are usually very reasonable and flexible, but mistakes do happen, and one has few avenues for recourse here, so it pays to be a little circumspect. Good places to start a shopping safari are the main streets of Ubud—Monkey Forest Road, Jalan Raya and Jalan Hanoman—and the 'handicrafts highway' which runs north from Ubud through Andong to the towns of Sebatu and Pujung. This road offers almost 20 km (12 miles) of non-stop craft shopping, and it is where many professional buyers from overseas retailers do their shopping for export. The mix of items for sale along this road is so entertaining that it's worth the drive, even if you don't want to buy a thing.

Moving upmarket, the road leading from Ubud northwest to Sayan offers excellent shopping, with a focus on furniture and home accessories as well as antiques and artworks. Pushing the upper-end envelope still further are a number of shops along the Sayan road between the Amandari Hotel and the Four Seasons, with exquisite gifts, houseware, jewellery, baskets and intriguing artefacts from various parts of Asia. The gift shops of the ultra-elite hotels in this area are also excellent spots to shop.

laid-back spas and powered up sports

You can go to almost any extreme in central and east Bali, from laid-back to powered up. The spas of Bali's heartland, located in and around the best hotels, are among the best in the world, with an exceptional range of services, plus that indescribably delightful Balinese touch—so gracious and ethereal that you'll think you've died and gone to heaven. This is the place to be if you feel the need to relax and let everything go, surrendering your body to therapeutic pampering. There are daily meditation and yoga sessions offered at various places in Ubud as well. But if a completely spa-focused holiday is what you're after, check into one of the spas located in the verdant hills of Ubud such as Kirana Spa and Bagus Jati

At the far end of the spectrum, central and east Bali are loaded with all sorts of sports, adventure and new experiences. The town of Taro has an elephant park where

you can ride (and bathe) elephants or simply watch them. A riding stable near Ubud offers opportunities for invigorating canters through the hills, and several companies are adept at organising exciting river rafting and mountain biking tours, four-wheel drive adventures, guided treks and even bird-watching walks. You can also just check with your hotel because most of them will offer similar tours, guides or services that allow you to enjoy the best of Bali's great outdoors. There's just so much at your fingertips that you'll find it hard to fit everything you want to do into one trip here.

an early night in the heartlands

Although there is plenty to do during the day, the interior and east of Bali have no hot spots when it comes to nightlife. Ubudians treasure their traditional atmosphere and consequently nightclubs are not allowed. The situation outside Ubud, in the more remote areas, is even quieter still. There are a few bars in Ubud with music, foremost among which are Jazz Café and Café Exiles, but the main form of entertainment is still traditional performances and ceremonies, available in abundance, complemented by excellent dining and good conversation.

Dining out in Ubud is a tremendous problem because there is just too much to choose from—posing a real challenge—with the quality of the better known restaurants ranging from reliably good to truly outstanding. There are charming cafés with superlative coffees and cakes, trendy sidewalk bistros, high-end eateries and chic restaurants serving all manner of Asian and international cuisines. In addition to excellent food, prices are also very affordable, so don't decide to go on a diet while in Ubud. Outside the environs of Ubud, there's hardly a thing for the selective palate, with the notable exception of a couple of superb hotels and a few remote retreats, or Kedai, a lovely beachside café in Candidasa, east Bali. So plan accordingly if you are a selective eater, or you may have to settle for snacks and fresh fruit from roadside stalls for the duration of your stay.

THIS PAGE (FROM TOP): Views over the Ayung River are never better than when seen from this pavilion at Alila Ubud; a floral footbath at Bagus Jati followed by foot reflexology illustrates why central Bali is known as a centre for healing and rejuvenation. OPPOSITE: This massage pavilion at Kirana Spa is the perfect place to be at the end of a day spent exploring central Bali.

The spas of Bali's heartland...are among the best in the world...

Alila Ubud

Alila Ubud sits on a hillside high above the Ayung River valley, just a short drive from Bali's legendary artistic centre, Ubud.

This beautiful retreat, with its traditional Balinese architecture, neatly thatched roofs, secluded courtyards and private gardens, was designed to merge with and enhance its natural setting. It offers a unique blend of timeless charm and elegant modernity.

Against a lush, palm-covered slope, the resort's 56 rooms are housed in two-storey blocks facing the valley and mountain range. Those on the ground floor feature garden terraces and open-air private showers, while those upstairs have a wide balcony with panoramic views.

Of the eight villas available, the four Ayung River Villas offer a spacious walk-around deck that looks over the valley below, while the remaining Garden Villas feature private tropical gardens and outdoor baths surrounded by calm lotus ponds.

Warm, contemporary colours and the use of local materials such as coconut wood create a tranquil and intimate mood inside that complements the spectacular views of the Ayung River valley below.

In a large Balinese pavilion, Alila Ubud's fabulous restaurant artfully combines Mediterranean and Asian cuisines, serving a sophisticated menu that includes inspired dishes like Spiced Pumpkin Soup with Crispy

Prawn Wontons, or Steamed Snapper in Saffron Lemon Grass Broth with Soba Noodles, Mussels and Snow Peas.

This cosy resort also has one of Bali's most amazing swimming pools. That's quite an achievement for an island with more than its fair share of inviting examples. Voted one of the '50 Most Spectacular Pools in the World' by *Travel + Leisure*, this solid body of water juts out over the Ayung River like a slab of liquid onyx, disturbed only as you dive into its welcoming waters.

If, like the Balinese, you consider your body a 'temple', then reward it with a visit to the resort's Mandara Spa, a destination that is pure indulgence for the mind, body and spirit. Immerse yourself in a series of sensual rites and balancing body rituals to restore, revive and re-energise your senses. Part of your daily journey to well-being can include a private yoga session at sunset in the Balinese bengong poised high above the valley. You may also choose to purify your mind with an hour of Tai Chi at sunrise, or simply take in the scenery with an early morning walk in the valley.

Don't be surprised if you find the resort hosting a wedding while you're there. Alila Ubud, like its sister property, Alila Manggis, is a popular spot with couples looking for a

THIS PAGE AND OPPOSITE: The hotel's swimming pool exudes a stillness matched by its surroundings.

ceremony that blesses the union in the magical style of the island. The whole ceremony takes place against the area's awe-inspiring natural backdrop.

Should you choose to spend your time at Alila Ubud experiencing more of Bali's famed culture, you may wish to join one of the hotel's personalised tours and workshops that lead you through the island's world of religious devotion, natural beauty, and social and cultural mores. Choose from classes covering Balinese architecture, the music of the gamelan, local dance, batik or history, all of which will arouse your curiosity and deepen your understanding of this extraordinary and unique island.

The more adventurous among you might prefer indulging in a little river rafting on

THIS PAGE (FROM TOP):
*The poolside cabana offers
a varied menu;
friendly service is all around.*
OPPOSITE (CLOCKWISE FROM TOP LEFT):
*A wantilan houses the
property's restaurant;
modern Balinese style defines
the comfortable rooms;
indulge your senses at the
resort's Mandara Spa.*

picture-perfect ceremony and reception, and for good reason. The resort can organise a number of themed weddings ranging from a contemporary celebration in white linen, to a tropical garden filled with orchids. Following a legal ceremony that ensures your marriage is recognised around the world, couples may choose to honour the event the local way with a Balinese Hindu

the Ayung, mountain biking along a downhill trail from Mount Batur, or a three-and-a-half-hour trek along the nearby valley that ends with a picnic by the river. These activities offer the perfect opportunity to enjoy the area's natural charm.

Alila Ubud, with its combination of astonishing beauty, cultural richness and friendly faces, is definitely a one-stop retreat for those who want to experience a little bit of everything Bali has to offer, and perhaps, a whole lot more.

FACTS

ROOMS	56 rooms • 8 villas
FOOD	restaurant: Asian and Mediterranean
DRINK	poolside cabana
FEATURES	pool • spa
BUSINESS	2 meeting rooms
NEARBY	Ubud centre • shopping • biking • river rafting
CONTACT	Desa Melinggih Kelod, Payangan, Ubud 80572 • telephone: +62.361.975 963 • facsimile: +62.361.975 968 • email: ubud@alilahotels.com • website: www.alilahotels.com

PHOTOGRAPHS COURTESY OF ALILA UBUD.

Alila Manggis

Head away from the crowds for the unspoiled east coast of Bali. There you'll find Alila Manggis, a gem of a boutique resort that combines the best of Bali's tropical landscape, the sea and the island's cultural diversity.

Inspired by the traditional Balinese wantilan and the royal water palace in the nearby village of Ujung, Alila Manggis features contemporary architecture that is in harmony with its natural surroundings. It is a serene hotel with a distinctive character, backed by gently cultivated rice fields and broad valleys, while the imposing Mount Agung beckons in the distance.

Four graceful Balinese pavilions with grass roofs and interlinked water gardens form a compound of 58 spacious rooms and suites, all with private terraces and day beds. From here, guests can enjoy uninterrupted views of the ocean.

Interiors have been influenced by the traditional colours of the culturally rich Bali Aga villages which are tucked away in the surrounding valleys. Hand-woven textiles, rattan, basketry and local woods such as coconut, have been used to maximum effect, incorporating comforting shades of honey, cream and chocolate—all of which reflect the hues of volcanic rock and sand.

The resort's lobby overlooks calming lotus ponds and a swimming pool set in a beautiful coconut grove where a beachfront

bale offers a restful retreat. Your options are simple: spend the day lazing beneath the trees by the pool, enjoy a good book while stretched out on your terrace, or indulge in a massage at the resort's spa.

Food is a way of life at Alila Manggis. Noted for its sumptuous meals, Seasalt, with views of the ocean and the pool, serves a menu featuring signature seafood dishes and regional specialities. If you find yourself utterly impressed with your meal, sign up for a cooking class at Alila Cooking School. Here, the resort's chefs will lead guests on an early-morning expedition to purchase

THIS PAGE: Alila's inviting pool is set within a quiet coconut grove just a few steps away from the beach, and ranks among the island's most picturesque.

OPPOSITE: Stylish yet relaxed, the resort's restaurant is in an open pavilion and is rightly famed for its modern Balinese cuisine.

the necessary ingredients for a delicious and authentic Balinese meal, before the lively outdoor lesson begins.

There's fun for divers too; the waters here offer some of the best scuba activity around, including an old shipwreck just 120 m (131 yd) off the beach. Geko Dive, the resort's dive partner, offers PADI-certified dive masters and professional equipment. The area also offers an excellent opportunity for snorkelling and fishing.

Business is not entirely forgotten at Alila Manggis. With windows spanning the water gardens, two meeting rooms cater to groups of up to 30 and can also be used as a private dining area. The resort's comfortable library houses an extensive collection of reference books and novels, while a charming boutique displays the island's and region's handicrafts.

Alila Manggis is also a wonderfully romantic destination for a wedding. With its large expanse of manicured lawns, a central pool lit with floating candles, and a private beachfront garden, the hotel is a popular choice with couples looking to tie the knot.

East Bali is a region rich in tradition and culture. Recognising this, Alila Ubud offers many local excursions that provide valuable insights into Bali's complex and glorious heritage. The resort also has a series of workshops and tours designed to enhance your enjoyment of the area. These include a personalised tour of Klungkung Hall of Justice and Klungkung Art Museum to learn about the island's art and fabric design industries, and tours which introduce guests to interesting aspects of the local culture such as astrology, community and local history.

Taking an elegant approach to tourist accommodation in Bali and offering the perfect alternative to the busier southern beach resorts, Alila Manggis is where you will experience another side of this fascinating island—one where inspired design meets grace and tranquillity.

THIS PAGE (FROM LEFT):
Guests can view the pool and lotus ponds from the lobby; the bedrooms reflect Alila's contemporary style.

OPPOSITE (FROM LEFT): Sumptuous satay and ocean-fresh seafood are just two of the items on Alila's flavour-filled menu; all rooms offer either a wide balcony and day bed upstairs, or a garden terrace below.

PHOTOGRAPHS COURTESY OF ALILA MANGGIS.

FACTS		
ROOMS	56 rooms • 2 suites	
FOOD	Seasalt: regional specialities, cuisine au naturelle and contemporary fine dining • Alila Cooking School: local	
DRINK	Lobby Lounge	
FEATURES	pool • spa • snorkelling • fishing • diving • biking • library	
BUSINESS	2 meeting rooms	
NEARBY	Candidasa • Tenganan Bali Aga village	
CONTACT	Buitan, Manggis, Karangasem 80871 • telephone: +62.363.410 11 • facsimile: +62.363.410 15 • email: manggis@alilahotels.com • website: www.alilahotels.com	

Bagus Jati

Situated about 30 minutes from Ubud, Bagus Jati is a health retreat for those eager to improve their physical and mental well-being, and anyone looking for a relaxing holiday. Its hillside location at a gentle 700 m (2297 yd) above sea level means guests will benefit from the brisk and invigorating mountain air, and the complete escape from urban life that Bagus Jati offers.

This natural landscape is also home to healing and medicinal plants including papayas, bananas, coconuts, mangoes and various herbs and spices, many of which are used in the resort's exotic spa treatments and invigorating spa cuisine.

Reflecting ancient Chakra principles, Bagus Jati's eight circular and beautifully furnished villas enjoy spectacular views of the surrounding countryside, from the misty mountains to the shadowy valleys teeming with vibrant, tropical greenery. They come fully equipped with jacuzzis and private treatment facilities, thus ensuring privacy.

Outside the villas are landscaped gardens with winding pathways leading to the restaurant which is furnished with leather

THIS PAGE: This health and well-being resort, and the rice fields that surround it, stand on land once occupied by ancient Hindu settlements.

OPPOSITE: Bagus Jati's circular villas have enough distance between them to offer seclusion and quietude.

and teak, and features an open fireplace to provide warm relief from the chilly mountain air in the evenings. As good health and well-being are the aims here, Surya Restaurant and Bar maintains different daily menus, all of which use the freshest produce, herbs and spices. The wide spread covers selections from Asian, Australian and European cuisines. Special meals can also be ordered to suit specific dietary requirements such as weight reduction. Guests can choose to dine in the restaurant, which seats 20, or in the comfort of their rooms. Over at Iswari Pool Snack Bar—Iswari translates to Valley of Enchantment in Bahasa Indonesia—guests can enjoy fresh fruit cocktails, juices, snacks or lunch right by the inviting swimming pool.

The focal point of Bagus Jati, however, is its spring water pool, around which tropical spa pavilions and private water gardens are scattered. The pool is where guests can tone their muscles with aqua-jogging and aqua-aerobics. Personal and group sessions are available daily.

Among the pavilions surrounding the pool are the fitness centre and the yoga and meditation hall. The latter is circular in shape, just like the villas, and is located within a bamboo forest. This inspirational space allows guests to go about their exercises in peace, while listening to the gentle sounds of the river below. Guests can

immerse themselves in deep meditation under the instruction of professional yoga and pilates coaches. These sessions should be organised to coincide with the rising or setting of the sun, as this accentuates the natural rhythms and cycles that drive our bodies. The exposure to pilates is particularly beneficial to those who spend far too much time hunched in front of a computer screen, or gripping the steering wheel of a vehicle. These short lessons can ease the burden on your spine.

For more intense physical activity, the Bagus Jati fitness centre offers state-of-the-art gym equipment including cardiovascular machines to monitor your heart rate. The fitness centre is housed in another circular pavilion that offers 180-degree views of the jungle. Those who enjoy outdoor workouts will appreciate the fitness trail, designed to facilitate jogging, brisk walks and various interval training routines.

To soothe your tired body at the end of the day, indulge in Bagus Jati's range of elaborate spa treatments which include Ayurvedic massage rituals, traditional Javanese flower baths with hydrotherapy, herbal steam baths, acupuncture, mud

THIS PAGE (CLOCKWISE FROM RIGHT): *Fresh fruits and plants are used in the resort's spa treatments and cuisine; tastefully furnished rooms ensure a comfortable stay; the spa treatment menu will leave you spoiled for choice.*
OPPOSITE: *Rest and relax with views of the countryside.*

wraps and more; all of which can be adapted to suit specific needs such as muscle aches, anti-aging, cell renewal, detoxification or just relaxation.

When you feel the need to step outside the property, you'll find a number of noteworthy attractions nearby. At the top of the list is Jati River Holy Waterfall. Follow the short cut from the resort's main path: you'll discover a stream flowing over rocks covered with ferns and tropical trees,

heading towards the river below, where a natural swimming pool has been created around the waterfall for Bagus Jati's guests.

Guided tours can also be arranged to visit the local woodcarvers and stone sculptors at work producing their respective crafts with a look and mood unique to this region. Also of interest is Taro village, where you can view a breed of sacred and rare white cows, indigenous to this area. All these sights can be accommodated with a

carefully co-ordinated bicycle tour, provided you're fit and game enough to peddle your way around this fascinating territory.

Should you feel an overwhelming urge to take a part of this resort's spirit of well-being home with you, there are personalised cooking classes under a Balinese chef that include a tour of the farm fields and spice gardens, as well as an introduction to the preparation involved when cooking a traditional Balinese feast.

FACTS		
	ROOMS	8 villas
	FOOD	Surya Restaurant and Bar: Asian and Western • special diets
	DRINK	Iswari Pool Snack Bar: fruit juices, cocktails, snacks and lunch
	FEATURES	yoga and meditation pavilion • spring water pool • in-room jacuzzi and treatment facility • cooking classes
	BUSINESS	operator-assisted calls
	NEARBY	Taro village • Ubud centre
	CONTACT	Desa Sebatu, Kecamatan Tegallalang, PO Box 4, Ubud 80572 • telephone: +62.361.978 885 • facsimile: +62.361.974 666 • email: info@bagusjati.com • website: www.bagusjati.com

PHOTOGRAPHS COURTESY OF BAGUS JATI.

The Chedi Club at Tanah Gajah

THIS PAGE: The outdoor bathtub in the Pool Villa is flanked by small ponds.

OPPOSITE (FROM TOP): Guests can survey their surroundings from the main pool; the open-air dining pavilion enjoys gentle breezes and views of the rice fields.

The Chedi Club at Tanah Gajah has gone to great lengths to ensure its guests experience the most restful retreat possible. The resort sprawls over five hectares (12 acres), with beautifully landscaped gardens that create an inviting and idyllic holiday mood. Just beyond its boundaries, the sight of endlessly rolling rice fields stretching out into the distance gives guests immediate assurance that they will certainly enjoy all the privacy that they wish for. In fact, The Chedi Club will quickly come to feel like the exclusive family home it once was.

The estate on which the resort stands is known locally as Tanah Gajah. Built by Hendra Hadiprana, a prominent Indonesian architect and interior designer, the property was originally used as a weekend retreat for his family and friends. These days, however, The Chedi Club is run by the GHM group which is also responsible for The Legian and The Club at The Legian. This accounts for

...The Chedi Club will quickly come to feel like the exclusive family home it once was.

the most sincere and engaging marriage of personalised care and professional service that guests tend to encounter here.

The Chedi Club is located along the lush and fertile stretch of land between the Petanu and Pakrisan rivers, and takes its name from the nearby Goa Gajah elephant temple. To match the cultural and historical feel of its surroundings, the rooms at The Chedi Club feature an extensive collection of local handcrafted furniture and authentic Balinese artefacts. These were provided by the Hadiprana Gallery and Boutique which houses the renowned Hadiprana collection. A selection of local souvenirs and books are also available for purchase here.

The resort has 20 assorted rooms, all of which come fully equipped with the usual comforts and indulgences so you won't have to take a single step outside to feel thoroughly pampered. The rooms available include one-bedroom Spa Villas, Pool Villas and suites, and a two-bedroom Estate Villa that makes for an exceptionally memorable stay. Tastefully decorated throughout, the interiors highlight the design team's sophisticated application and interpretation of traditional Balinese artistic styles.

Indeed, guests will appreciate the strong sense of creative passion that runs through the landscape as well, as is evident in the thoughtful arrangement of mature

trees, calm lotus ponds and the presence of a lovely ornamental lake, all of which have been carefully tended to for over 20 years.

Each room is assigned a private butler dedicated to ensuring that guests enjoy the most satisfying resort experience possible. This service does not exclude guests who choose the suites, thus leaving The Chedi Club in a class of its own when it comes to making each and every guest feel equally important. For an even more privileged time, opt for one of the private Spa Villas which feature a personal sauna, a cold plunge pool, an indoor and outdoor bathroom, and

a massage suite. Enjoying exclusive access to these facilities is a luxury effectively enhanced by unhurried spa treatments, performed by professional therapists, that will leave you feeling utterly relaxed and contented, all within the private world of your spacious and comfortable villa.

On the other hand, those looking forward to lapping up the sun will prefer one of the Pool Villas, each with its own swimming pool and deck, in addition to a dining bale set against a walled tropical garden. Here, guests can work up a robust appetite while getting thoroughly acquainted

THIS PAGE (CLOCKWISE FROM RIGHT): The luxurious Pool Villa offers guests a private retreat with its own dining pavilion; the living room of the Spa Villa overlooks the resort's tropical garden; handcrafted furniture is a distinguishing feature of The Chedi Club.
OPPOSITE: The Spa Villas offer spacious semi-outdoor bathrooms with large bathtubs, a 'rainforest-spa shower', sauna and cold plunge pool.

with the lovely Balinese weather. To enjoy a little pampering of the body and mind, guests will have to visit the spa, where an extensive menu of soothing natural therapies and treatments, private yoga sessions in the roomy meditation studio, and sweeping, panoramic views of the countryside await.

Dining is an open-air affair at The Restaurant and Club Lounge, jointly located in a huge pavilion set against the backdrop of verdant rice fields and the legendary Mount Agung. The main restaurant offers traditional Balinese cuisine prepared in an open kitchen. This allows mouth-watering aromas to drift towards appreciative diners. Guests will be pleased to know that the supply of ducks, chickens, vegetables and herbs used in the recipes are obtained from organic farms around Bali, and these ensure a healthy and wholesome diet during your stay at The Chedi Club.

Right beside The Restaurant is the Club Lounge, where a cosy arrangement of day beds allows guests to enjoy their afternoon tea or evening cocktails in a relaxed and comfortable setting. There's also the option of enjoying speciality cocktails and a fine selection of cigars at the nearby Bird Lounge, a nature-lover's sanctuary that overlooks the main aviary of Tanah Gajah. Here, guests can bury their noses in a wide collection of illustrated books about birds.

The heart of Ubud is a short walk away and offers all sorts of cultural and shopping distractions. Those who would rather not walk can opt to use the resort's convenient limousine service. This is especially handy for those planning to buy bulky artwork.

With such attention to service, you can rest assured every detail will be taken care of for you at The Chedi Club.

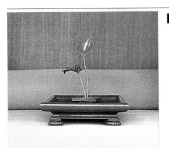

FACTS

ROOMS	7 suites • 3 Spa Villas • 9 Pool Villas • 1 Estate Villa
FOOD	The Restaurant: Balinese • The Pool Pavilion: light snacks
DRINK	Club Lounge: cocktails and afternoon tea • The Bird Lounge: cocktails and cigars
FEATURES	pool • spa • gym • yoga • The Hadiprana Gallery and Boutique • tennis
BUSINESS	boardroom
NEARBY	Ubud centre • Mount Agung • trekking
CONTACT	Jalan Goa Gajah, Tengkulak Kaja, Ubud 80571 • telephone: +62.361.975.685 • facsimile: +62.361.975.686 • email: resort@thechediclububud.com • website: www.ghmhotels.com

PHOTOGRAPHS COURTESY OF THE CHEDI CLUB AT TANAH GAJAH.

Ibah Luxury Villas

As one of the area's more established boutique hotels, Ibah Luxury Villas dominates its lush and hilly natural surroundings with a distinguished air. Though its new buildings were constructed on the former site of the Tjetjak Inn as recently as 1995, they have been crafted with a majestic and meditative style reminiscent of holy temple retreats. It is thus a real luxury, as the name implies, to seek solace within these walls.

Situated at the convergence of the rivers Oos and Campuhan, the land on which Ibah is located has been handed down through the centuries from one generation of the Ubud royal family to another. In fact, these unique villas owe their design and construction to a descendant of the royal court. Fittingly, the name 'Ibah' means 'bequest' in Bahasa Indonesia, and it will quickly strike guests during a stay here that they have indeed been presented with a truly special hotel retreat.

Ibah Luxury Villas is especially popular with lovers of native arts and artefacts for the way it integrates antique furnishings and accessories with its décor. The grounds of

*THIS PAGE AND OPPOSITE: **The pool's design, with private, shady caves to lounge in, brings to mind ancient Balinese temples.***

this hotel also express a deep appreciation for Balinese country life and its close association with nature. Many of the villas' thatched, elephant grass roofs feature traditional ornaments embellished with characters from the animal world such as bulls and snakes. These are made from the black fibre of the jaka palm tree, locally known as ijuk. Inside, woven bamboo mats cover the ceilings. Such details testify to the dedicated handiwork and craftsmanship that were necessarily involved.

Ibah's 15 villas are named after various flowers and are decorated with lovely ceramics and earthenware utensils. Most of the villas also feature beautiful Javanese glass paintings. Villa Frangipani is a modest mansion with two bedrooms. Step inside and you'll be greeted by a waterfall, from where you'll find a flight of stairs leading up to a pavilion housing a dining room, large day bed, fully stocked mini-bar and a sound system: perfect for a day spent indoors. The two bedrooms are separated by a pool that overlooks the Campuhan valley.

The deluxe suite, Villa Allamanda, on the other hand, is approached by crossing a bridge where stone animal figures spout fountains of water. They lead to an arch with antique carved wooden pillars marking the entrance of the suite. A four-poster bed with a canopy of mosquito net curtains has pride

of place here. Step out onto the balcony and you'll find a cosy living room with views of the surrounding countryside.

To enter Villa Rose, also known as the honeymoon suite, guests must ascend a spiral staircase leading to a room featuring antique carvings along the ceiling.

A more recent addition is Treetops, an extension that houses four suites situated to provide views of the rainforest and river below. The building is actually accessed through an imaginative white stone structure designed to suggest a cave entrance. A flight of stairs leads to a pair of Deluxe Suites above, and Standard Suites below. Various ink illustrations, glass paintings and ceramics add a touch of class. Coupled with

wooden shingles on its roof, terrazzo floors and marble bathrooms, Treetops adds to Ibah's secluded charm.

Those who enjoy the great outdoors will find much pleasure in river rafting, mountain biking and trekking: activities which Ibah can easily organise. Culture-seekers, on the other hand, will appreciate tours of Ubud and the neighbouring villages. In fact, Ibah is so conveniently located that whether you're enjoying a stroll along the banks of the Campuhan, or exploring central Ubud and its many shops and restaurants, you're always within walking distance of the hotel.

Those who would much rather enjoy the hotel's facilities might take a dip in the saltwater swimming pool, or relax in their

THIS PAGE (CLOCKWISE FROM RIGHT):
Four-poster beds feature in each villa; dining outdoors is a relaxing and intimate experience; cosy walkways with high stone walls add to the feeling of being sheltered from the outside world.

OPPOSITE: Guests can enjoy spa treatments in enclosed courtyards filled with tropical plants.

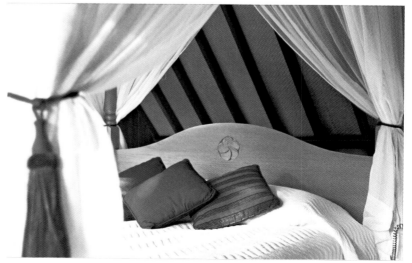

villa with a selection of books or music from the library. Regular Tai Chi sessions help to keep guests physically and psychologically centred throughout their stay. Alternatively, group or personal yoga sessions can be arranged. Cool down after these sessions with a relaxing massage or other healing treatments and therapies at Ibah's spa.

Guests won't even have to leave the hotel for a great meal as The Restaurant and Bar offer an intimate experience in a pavilion surrounded by fish ponds and gently flowing water. Here, you can feast on modern Asian cuisine, grilled seafood and meat, pasta specialities and traditional Indonesian dishes. After a satisfying meal, adjourn to the cigar and whiskey lounge for a relaxing drink before bedtime.

Ibah Luxury Villas is a cosy hotel that offers five-star service and facilities. This makes it a popular choice with travellers looking for a little more privacy but with all the perks of a larger hotel.

PHOTOGRAPHS COURTESY OF IBAH LUXURY VILLAS.

FACTS		
ROOMS	1 two-bedroom Pool Villa • 1 one-bedroom Pool Villa • 2 Ibah Suites • 9 Deluxe Suites • 2 Standard Suites	
FOOD	The Restaurant and Bar: Indonesian and Asian	
DRINK	Tembako Cigar and Whiskey Lounge	
FEATURES	spa • pool • library • cultural tours • trekking • biking • river rafting	
BUSINESS	meeting room	
NEARBY	Ubud centre • Gunung Lebah • holy springs	
CONTACT	Puri Tjampuhan, Ubud 80571 • telephone: +62.361.974 466 • facsimile: +62.361.974 467 • email: ibah@dps.centrin.net.id • website: www.ibahbali.com	

Komaneka Resort

Located deep in the heart of downtown Ubud, Komaneka Resort is an unexpected retreat amidst the never-ending hustle and bustle. Stroll through the resort's expansive grounds, with its thick, tropical vegetation and abundant arrangement of exotic plants, and you'll feel a world away from the lively scene of restaurants, shops, museums and galleries just a short walk down the road from its gate. Despite its central location, Komaneka Resort offers as much privacy and exclusivity as its sister property nearby, Komaneka Tanggayuda.

A number of Pool Villas, Garden Villas, Suite Rooms and Deluxe Rooms make up the resort. All of them share similar amenities such as a king-size bed (or twin beds in the Deluxe Rooms), a sunken marble bathtub with a separate shower, and a private verandah. Each room features locally crafted furnishings draped in soft, earth-toned fabrics. In fact, aside from the private plunge pool that comes with the Pool Villa, the only differences between the rooms are their size and the views they offer. An infinity-edged main pool is available for all guests.

The Garden Terrace Restaurant serves contemporary Indonesian and international cuisine throughout the day, and seats up to 30 diners with ease. The extensive menu offers hearty breakfasts and a selection of lunch and dinner specials that will satisfy all palates. Over at the Pool Bar, guests can enjoy a light lunch or that essential evening aperitif, with a selection of wines, spirits and cocktails to choose from.

Komaneka Resort's spa will help counter the inevitable exhaustion following a day spent exploring Ubud's many offerings with its range of traditional Indonesian beauty and massage treatments. The spa has been designed to accommodate both couples, with a choice of open-air treatment rooms, and individuals, who might prefer to unwind

in complete privacy. The deeply relaxing treatments you can expect include Balinese massages, herbal body scrubs and wraps, and Indonesian-style herbal baths.

Guests who want to enjoy the outdoors can organise river rafting and diving expeditions through the resort, and visits to Bali's many historical sites and renowned museums and galleries, such as the Neka Art Museum. In fact, the resort's fine art gallery and gift shop are managed by the family that founded the Neka Art Museum. This direct link to Bali's cultural legacy will surely appeal to the art connoisseur in you.

THIS PAGE: The rooms overlook rice fields or the garden.

OPPOSITE (FROM TOP): Wandering around the tropical grounds, guests will forget that the busy centre of Ubud is a short walk away; the main pool is where guests can enjoy a leisurely swim or a refreshing drink at the Pool Bar.

FACTS		
	ROOMS	4 Pool Villas • 2 Garden Villas • 2 Suite Rooms • 12 Deluxe Rooms
	FOOD	Garden Terrace Restaurant: contemporary Indonesian and international
	DRINK	Pool Bar: light lunch and refreshments
	FEATURES	pool • spa • fine art gallery • gift shop • library with satellite television
	BUSINESS	IDD telephone
	NEARBY	Neka Art Museum • Museum Puri Lukisan • Monkey Forest • cafés • restaurants
	CONTACT	Jalan Monkey Forest, Ubud 80571 • telephone: +62.361.976 090 • facsimile: +62.361.977 140 • email: sales@komaneka.com • website: www.komaneka.com

PHOTOGRAPHS COURTESY OF KOMANEKA RESORT.

Komaneka Tanggayuda

The location is absolutely tranquil, and the unhampered view over the River Oos is precisely the stuff to write home about. That's the essence of Komaneka Tanggayuda, a cosy resort in the village of Kedewatan, near Ubud. Given that its sister property is Komaneka Resort, guests can definitely expect the same degree of luxury and painstaking attention paid to design details that mark the former. Here, many simple touches, such as the local artefacts that liven up every corner of the property, help to make your stay a memorable experience.

The resort's exterior has been designed to reflect the terraced natural environment all around, and its interior is just as elaborate and distinctive. The primary aim was to maximise guests' encounter with Bali's many natural blessings by leaving entrances and views as open as possible.

The Valley Pool Villas offer spectacular vistas of the river valley below in addition to all the usual comforts such as a private plunge pool, an intricately carved volcanic stone bathtub, cosy day beds, a private verandah, a king-size bed and a pavilion suitable for intimate meals. The Courtyard Pool Villas are packaged similarly but enjoy different views. The Suite Rooms are just as luxurious, but guests who select these rooms

will have to use the resort's infinity-edged pool which overlooks the river valley.

When it is time to dine, Warung Kudus will surpass your expectations with its mix of contemporary Indonesian and international cuisines. The restaurant is housed in an old building displaying traditional Balinese design with exquisite handcrafted wood panels and details. Guests can enjoy all their meals here or head to the Terrace Café for a light lunch and refreshments.

Based near Bali's artistic hub, Ubud, it should come as no surprise that the resort has a fine art gallery with a collection of contemporary art by both international and local talents. The gift shop is another popular spot, with antiques, clothing, jewellery and other Indonesian arts and crafts available for your appreciation and purchase. For even more variety, hop on the resort's shuttle service to Ubud and take your pick from the many galleries there.

THIS PAGE: Private plunge pools and cosy outdoor pavilions feature in each villa.

OPPOSITE (FROM TOP): The main pool, surrounded by lush vegetation, overlooks the river valley; details matter in the resort's lobby, where an inviting day bed to rest on while your room is prepared, makes a memorable difference.

FACTS

ROOMS	8 Valley Pool Villas • 8 Courtyard Pool Villas • 4 Suite Rooms
FOOD	Warung Kudus: Indonesian and international
DRINK	Terrace Café: light lunch and refreshments
FEATURES	pool • spa • fine art gallery • gift shop • library with satellite television
BUSINESS	IDD telephone
NEARBY	Ubud Market • Monkey Forest • Puri Saren
CONTACT	Banjar Tanggayuda, Kedewatan, Ubud 80571 • telephone: +62.361.978 123 • facsimile: +62.361.973 084 • email: sales@komaneka.com • website: www.komaneka.com

PHOTOGRAPHS COURTESY OF KOMANEKA TANGGAYUDA.

Maya Ubud Resort + Spa

Maya Ubud Resort and Spa can be found nestled along the banks of the Petanu River, and in close proximity to the villages of Bedulu and Pejeng. It sits on 10 hectares (25 acres) of verdant hillside with a garden-like atmosphere that surrounds its rooms and private villas. Both are positioned to enjoy spectacular views which extend over the river or lush rice terraces.

Here, weather-beaten timbers and natural materials are brought together in a novel manner. Maya Ubud's award-winning architect Budiman Hendropurnomo has designed a resort that combines new and old in a striking manner. The classic Balinese style is captured on the exterior largely through the extensive use of thatched roofs and pavilion-like buildings, while the interiors are brought to life with elements that are rich with local character and unique in design. Wheels from old farm carts have been creatively reworked to serve as frames for mirrors, while teak railway sleepers have been recycled into sturdy table tops. Similarly, traditional fish traps and baskets have been modified to create beautiful handcrafted lamp shades.

This homage to historical Bali, through the inventive use of traditional items, is most strongly expressed in spaces such as the expansive lobby, restaurants and rooms which have a cosy, elegant feel coupled with clean, contemporary lines.

The resort has a number of rooms with balconies to choose from, along with Garden Villas, Pool Villas, Duplex Villas and a Presidential Villa. Every villa features a private garden, and each room comes with either a luxurious king-size bed or two single beds. The Garden Villas, in particular, offer even more space with a terrace that affords exceptional views of the surrounding area. In addition, the Pool Villas, Duplex Villas and Presidential Villa feature private plunge

THIS PAGE: The villas are tucked into the lush hillside.

OPPOSITE (FROM TOP): Besides a private pool and deck, each villa is surrounded by a landscaped garden; guests can enjoy leisurely treks through the rice fields.

...a resort that combines new and old in a striking manner.

pools which offer complete exclusivity accompanied by a relaxed mood.

Culinary treats abound at Maya Ubud. Guests have a choice of dining at the in-house restaurant, Maya Sari Mas, the more breezy River Café, or the hip and stylish Bar Bedulu. The menu at Maya Sari presents an exciting range of the region's spicy cuisine, and lunch delights include intriguing starters like the Tuna Medallion served on a bed of rocket, romaine and anchovies tossed with sun-dried tomatoes and olives, hearty soups like the Tom Yam Goong (a Thai broth of prawns and garoupa), and a number of sumptuous main dishes such as the Sweet and Sour Garoupa Fillet served with pineapple and jasmine rice, and the Green Thai Duck Curry with ginger relish, steamed

rice and fresh coriander. These creations are best enjoyed on the uncovered dining terrace set by the hillside, with views of the Petanu River stretching out below diners. The River Café, on the other hand, is perfect for less formal gatherings, and offers a fuss-free riverside dining experience just above the spa and its adjoining swimming pool. Here, guests can savour the specialities that make up the resort's spa cuisine.

Bar Bedulu, next to the lobby, offers a refreshing selection of tropical cocktails and fresh fruit juices, as well as the perennial favourite, ice-cold beer. An array of tempting snacks also feature at the bar. Two highly recommended items are the Lebanese Eggplant and Chickpea Tartar served with red pepper pesto and smoked marlin, and the Duck and Shitake Spring Rolls which come with beetroot chutney and cucumber noodles. A private candlelit dinner in your villa makes for a more intimate alternative.

There is also much to do at Maya Ubud itself. River rafting, yoga, tennis, swimming, trekking and biking in the lush countryside are just some of the many ways guests can enjoy the resort and the beauty of its surroundings. Culture-seekers will spend a lot of time by the amphitheatre next to Maya Sari Mas as colourful cultural performances

THIS PAGE (CLOCKWISE FROM RIGHT):
Even with twin beds, the rooms maintain their spacious, airy feel; the dining experience at River Café is enhanced by stunning views; guests can unwind in an infinity-edged pool.
OPPOSITE: Enjoy evening cocktails at the main pool served by the friendly staff of Bar Bedulu.

by troupes from the neighbouring villages are regularly performed here. Bali has long been known for its vibrant arts scene and its community of expatriate and local artists, and introductory painting lessons give guests a hands-on experience of the island's lively creative activities. Biking trails bring guests closer to local culture, archaeological ruins, natural attractions, temples and historical sites. A particularly popular trail takes you into the homes of local woodcarvers, painters and craftsmen to witness the dedication with which they ply their trade. Off the bikes, you can also walk into Ubud and take in the sights and sounds of Bali's artistic and cultural centre.

To help you unwind after a day spent outdoors, indulge in a visit to the Spa at Maya, a riverside haven of peace and tranquillity where guests can get close to nature while enjoying invigorating and exotic treatments in complete privacy. The single or double treatment pavilions along the picturesque riverbank feature views of the rainforest in all its untamed beauty, forming a perfect backdrop against which you can enjoy a massage to end the day.

FACTS		
	ROOMS	36 Superior Rooms • 12 Deluxe Rooms • 23 Garden Villas • 34 Pool Villas • 1 Pejeng Duplex Villa • 1 Peliatan Duplex Villa • 1 Petanu Presidential Villa
	FOOD	Maya Sari Mas: Asian and international • Maya Sari Asiatique: Asian, with teppanyaki counter • River Café: spa cuisine, salads and light snacks
	DRINK	Bar Bedulu: cocktails, fruit juices and light snacks
	FEATURES	pool • spa • tennis • trekking • river rafting • cultural tours • yoga • biking
	BUSINESS	meeting and banquet facilities
	NEARBY	Ubud centre • museums • galleries • cafés • restaurants
	CONTACT	Jalan Gunung Sari, Peliatan, Ubud 80571 • telephone: +62.361.977 888 • facsimile: +62.361.977 555 • email: info@mayaubud.com • website: www.mayaubud.com

PHOTOGRAPHS COURTESY OF MAYA UBUD RESORT AND SPA.

Natura Resort + Spa

Natura Resort and Spa is a sanctuary located just outside the centre of Ubud, and is accessed through the quiet village of Laplapan that seems little touched or changed by time. The resort's architects designed Natura with special consideration shown to the area's natural environment. As a result, its luxury villas were built to blend unobtrusively into the landscape, thus rendering a seamless meeting of nature and architecture to most beautiful effect.

Based on the vision of Popo Danes, one of Bali's more prominent local architects, each villa faces the west so that guests can enjoy beautiful sunsets every evening, and sweeping views of the Petanu River that flows alongside. Natura's 14 luxury villas line the edge of the river valley and this

THIS PAGE AND OPPOSITE (MAIN PICTURE):
The resort's terraces were designed to match the topographical characteristics of the area.
BELOW: *The luxurious jacuzzi is one of many hydrotherapy facilities available here.*

accentuates its natural beauty without disturbing the environment or ecological balance in any significant way. The native vegetation, river and wildlife thus continue to flourish in their original state. Natura's preservation of nature has become an appealing feature that draws eco-tourists and environmentally-conscious travellers who appreciate the escape from the urban jungle into a scenic, lush haven.

Fully furnished and equipped, all villas offer the utmost privacy and feature an extensive use of natural materials and earth-tones to create a retreat-like ambience.

The three Traditional Villas resemble a walled Balinese village, each within its own compound. Guests enter through a gate leading to a front passageway and

proceed to a dining area with an adjoining bedroom and living room. The connecting marble bathroom leads to an appealing garden courtyard which offers perfect solitude. The four Deluxe Villas are available in single- or double-storey units with an indoor fibre bathtub and shower for the former, and an additional outdoor terrazzo bathtub and shower for the latter. While the duplex units include a king-size day bed, dining table and private garden, guests in the single-storey units enjoy a private wooden deck set in the treetops which commands an unobscured view of

the surrounding jungle terrain. The five Luxury Pool Villas are similar to the duplex Deluxe Villas, but with a notable exception—one of the villas was constructed with a more spacious living area and bedroom which open out onto a terrace with its own plunge pool overlooking the gardens and valley below. Last but not least are the two cosy villas with two bedrooms. One of these luxurious villas comes with a private jacuzzi, kitchenette and study, while the other is a duplex villa featuring a day bed, private plunge pool and tropical gardens on its lower level. All the villas ensure your privacy.

The Wantilan Restaurant offers an international menu and local treats. Of particular interest to foreign guests is the traditional Bebek Betutu (or Balinese Roasted Duck) set dinner. A local speciality, this dish is usually served to mark festive and religious celebrations as well as significant passage-of-life rituals such as tooth-filing, wedding ceremonies and funeral rites. At The Wantilan Restaurant, guests begin this important meal with a welcome drink of red or white French wine, followed by a hot appetiser of Sate Lilit Bebek, which is essentially aromatic grilled minced duck on a lemon grass skewer. Sup Pulung, a hot and spicy broth filled with duck dumplings follows. Finally, the main course of Bebek Betutu arrives. This dish consists of a tender roasted duckling wrapped in banana leaves, served with green vegetables and a selection of spicy Balinese dips.

All this can be enjoyed with fragrant Nasi Uduk (garlic and pandan rice) on the side, and some Urapan Bali (vegetable salad with steamed coconut shreds, chilli, palm sugar and kaffir lime) with assorted sambal preparations to spice up the flavours even more. For dessert, look forward to a traditional sweet concoction of stewed bananas in rich coconut milk with palm sugar syrup. End your meal with a cup of Calypso Coffee, a rich mix of espresso, rum,

THIS PAGE (CLOCKWISE FROM RIGHT): Large windows fill the spacious bedrooms with natural light; private plunge pools feature in some of the villas; wooden pathways wind their way gently through the resort's natural surroundings.
OPPOSITE: Scented and soothing, the traditional floral bath remains a novel treat for many.

crème de cacao and whipping cream. The Wantilan Bar, too, is well-stocked and is a relaxed location for post-dinner drinks.

The riverside spa offers traditional Balinese and Javanese beauty and healing rituals, conducted to the soothing trickle of flowing water. The natural springs offer a completely refreshing and rejuvenating experience, while two specially-designed massage rooms enhance the experience of these traditional remedies. A speciality here is the herbal clay treatment which involves smoothing a mixture of Indonesian herbs blended with a clay base all over your body. After a while, this treatment draws out toxins and helps to cleanse the body.

The charming Natura Resort and Spa is an environmentally aware retreat that offers guests the best of Balinese luxury along with all the modern amenities of a five-star resort, without sacrificing the very thing that makes Bali a hot favourite with travellers worldwide—its lush, tropical beauty.

PHOTOGRAPHS COURTESY OF NATURA RESORT AND SPA.

FACTS

ROOMS	3 Traditional Villas • 4 Deluxe Villas • 5 Luxury Pool Villas • 2 Two-Bedroom Villas
FOOD	The Wantilan Restaurant: Indonesian and international
DRINK	The Wantilan Bar and Lounge • Poolside Lounge
FEATURES	pool • spa • jacuzzi • sauna • gift shop • library • shuttle service to Ubud
BUSINESS	1 conference room
NEARBY	Ubud Palace • Monkey Forest • river rafting • elephant safari • biking • trekking • museums • galleries
CONTACT	Banjar Laplapan, Ubud 80571 • telephone: +62.361.978 666 • facsimile: +62.361.978 222 • email: natura@indosat.net.id • website: www.bali-natura.com

Pita Maha Resort + Spa

Set into the side of the Campuhan valley in Bali's cultural heartland, Ubud, Pita Maha Resort and Spa is a landscaped jewel overlooking the River Oos. The natural beauty of this setting is immediately apparent when you arrive; sweeping views of rice terraces and lush, green, tropical woodlands draw the eye along a verdant valley all the way to the south of Bali and the mesmerising sea beyond.

Established in 1995, Pita Maha was designed by a member of Ubud's royal family to commemorate the creation of a famous artistic movement that took shape during Bali's golden era of the 1930s. This movement was started in 1934 by Ubud's royal prince, Tjokorda Gde Agung Sukawati, in collaboration with celebrated artists Walter Spies and Rudolf Bonnet.

Referred to as 'Pita Maha' or 'Great Shining', the movement aimed to encourage the growth and development of local artists. As a result, it was directly responsible for the establishment of Ubud as Bali's cultural centre. Among the many talented artists who benefited from the 'Great Shining' were I Gusti Nyoman Lempad and Gusti Made Deblog. Their superb artwork is a testament to the vision and foresight of Spies, Bonnet and their royal benefactor.

Pita Maha displays a chic design to complement its royal ownership. Twenty-four

thatched villas are set in traditional, walled compounds amid rich, tropical gardens that fade into an impressive hillside backdrop and the Campuhan valley below.

Each compound comes equipped with an inviting plunge pool and tropical garden. Rooms in this completely private paradise are air-conditioned and stylishly fitted.

Guests with an eye for detail will revel in the local workmanship showcased in their beautiful wood and stone surroundings.

Outside, traditional bales and massage pavilions are scattered throughout the natural gardens which are linked by charming, fern-filled walkways. At the heart of this verdant universe is a stunning

THIS PAGE: *Spend the day floating above the verdant valley Oos in the enticing infinity-edged pool at Pita Maha.*

OPPOSITE: *Enjoy a massage in one of the open-air bales that dot the tropical gardens.*

THIS PAGE: *Guests are greeted at the lobby by magnificent views of neatly arranged rice terraces and lush woodlands, extending along the valley to the south and the sea beyond.*
OPPOSITE: *Unwind in a petal-strewn jacuzzi.*

infinity-edged pool that offers awe-inspiring views of the lush woodlands all around.

The same sense of space and light pervades the hotel's split-level restaurant which opens onto the scenic Campuhan valley and offers a delicious menu covering local and international dishes.

For a more relaxed setting—if that's even possible—there's an informal warung situated along spring water-fed pools in the resort's garden. Even here, Pita Maha offers a romantic retreat, excellent service and a taste of royal splendour.

Tucked away in the most secluded corner of the property, guests will find Pita Maha Private Villa Spa, offering a complete menu of health treatments in the most exquisite surroundings to ensure total

relaxation of body and mind. Choose from a menu that includes Balinese and herbal back massages, acupressure sessions or the traditional Indonesian Lulur treatment—a herbal body scrub accompanied by a refreshing yoghurt rub-down.

Equipped with every facility needed for the ultimate break, this luxurious spa in a villa also includes sauna and steam rooms that open onto hot or cold whirlpool baths, an eight-metre-long (26-ft-long) private pool, and a spring water plunge pool overflowing with fragrant tropical flowers. Open daily from 9 am, the villa can cater to couples or small groups of up to four people. Book the whole villa and you're assured of a very private spa experience.

The spa's enchanting, split-level design offers massage, aromatherapy and exotic herbal treatments in a private relaxation room, while an outdoor dining and leisure pavilion completes the experience of a perfect, healing hideaway.

PHOTOGRAPHS COURTESY OF PITA MAHA RESORT AND SPA.

FACTS		
	ROOMS	24 villas
	FOOD	Terrace Restaurant: local and international
	DRINK	Pool Side Bar
	FEATURES	pool • restaurant • spa
	BUSINESS	complimentary Internet access in the library
	NEARBY	shops • restaurants • bars
	CONTACT	Jalan Sanggingan, PO Box 198, Ubud 80571 • telephone: +62.361.974 330 • facsimile: +62.361.974 329 • email: pitamaha@indosat.net.id • website: www.pitamaha-bali.com

Puri Wulandari

THIS PAGE AND OPPOSITE (MAIN PICTURE):
The resort's main infinity-edged pool overlooks the Ayung River valley.

OPPOSITE (BELOW): *Steep drops, high walls and lush vegetation ensure seclusion and privacy.*

From the elegant terraces that line its poolside to the luxurious indoor and outdoor showers and the spa facilities within its compound, Puri Wulandari immediately strikes the first-time guest as a resort where exotic encounters might be experienced. Located in an area known for steep slopes, stunning views of the Ayung River valley and absolute seclusion, with little more than wide blue skies above and bountiful rice paddies all around to distract you, this resort offers a much-needed escape from the steel and concrete of the big city.

Puri Wulandari was designed to thrill the senses and excite the imagination. Its architecture is at once simple yet striking, and features natural woods that have been lovingly crafted into a series of cosy, inviting

pavilions and villas. The attention to detail and old-world charm of the resort suggests a style that is more reminiscent of the grand colonial mansions that once dotted the island rather than that of more contemporary establishments. Therefore, it should come as no surprise that Puri Wulandari is regarded as one of the finest luxury resorts in the area.

Three categories of villas—Srikandi, Drupadi and Maharani—are available here. All are tastefully accessorised and styled to create an intimate mood, and offer lavish facilities and services. Even the most jaded traveller will be warmed by personal attention from a team of butlers, all of whom are committed to enhancing your experience here. Every villa comes with a private

swimming pool, an outdoor living room and a sunken bathtub. Amenities such as a flat screen televsion, DVD and CD player, and a private bar allow guests to stay ensconced in their villas should they wish to do so.

Couples and those travelling alone will opt for the Srikandi Villas, of which there are 31. These are one-bedroom villas that come with a four-poster king-size bed. Only two of these villas do not have a private pool. The four Drupadi Villas have two bedrooms with king-size beds and are suitable for friends and small families. Both villas come with the option to switch to twin beds of course.

The magnificent and exclusive Maharani Villa is perfect for larger groups, with two master bedrooms, a jacuzzi, a kitchenette and a private room for the butler.

When mealtime arrives, there are two established restaurants here to choose from. Janger Restaurant is a fine-dining venue that is well-known in Bali's resort circle for its contemporary international cuisine. Here, guests can dine against the stunning backdrop of lush forests and lofty mountains. Offering a view that is just as enticing, Legong Terrace serves Mediterranean-Italian cuisine in a laid-back setting by the resort's

swimming pool. Both restaurants pay as much attention to visual presentation as they do to the delectable food.

As the sun makes its picturesque exit in the evening, make your way to Barong Bar where a refreshing cocktail can be enjoyed in the fading light. If you'd like to enjoy a quiet evening indoors, head to the library and select a book, DVD or CD to help you while away the rest of your day.

To start the day, on the other hand, you may like to indulge in a little pampering at Lila Ulangun Spa, a particularly impressive and comprehensive wellness centre that houses a gymnasium, hair and beauty salon, and two private treatment rooms, each with their own massage beds, plunge bath and sauna. Here, you can experience traditional Indonesian beauty and health rituals which use natural remedies that have survived the passage of time. One treatment that must be tried is the Balinese Honey Masque. First, a scented oil is massaged into your skin, lulling you into a peaceful nap, before a sea salt body scrub is applied to open your pores. A mixture of honey and sesame seeds is then smoothed over your body before you're wrapped in a warm blanket. This will help your body absorb the health benefits and moisturising qualities of the honey.

The traditional Balinese massage, a popular choice with guests, involves either a

dry massage that warms the body, or the application of thumb and palm pressure to ensure a therapeutic deep-tissue massage. A full-body Swedish massage, on the other hand, works by kneading the body in order to improve blood circulation and reduce tension, while the five aromatherapy oils used help to calm the body and harmonise physical and mental energies.

Hydrotherapy sessions are held in a deep bathtub constructed from natural white stone and fitted with underwater jets that gently massage your back and legs. Daily meditation sessions are also available for those seeking inner calm. To really get your heart pumping, head to the gymnasium.

Should you feel the need to leave the comforts of Puri Wulandari, make the most of its twice-daily shuttle bus service to and from Ubud. Travellers looking for a resort that offers luxury and seclusion while leaving them the option of a quick trip to town and other attractions nearby, will do well to choose Puri Wulandari.

THIS PAGE (FROM LEFT): The sunken bathtubs feature natural textures and materials; simple and elegant, the bedrooms showcase the resort's attention to detail; natural treatments based on traditional beauty secrets are delivered in modern comfort at the spa.

OPPOSITE: The pavilions are well-suited to meditation.

FACTS

ROOMS	31 Srikandi Villas • 4 Drupadi Villas • 1 Maharani Villa
FOOD	Janger Restaurant: modern international • Legong Terrace: Mediterranean-Italian
DRINK	Barong Bar
FEATURES	pool • spa • gymnasium • gift shop and gallery • library
BUSINESS	IDD telephone
NEARBY	Ubud centre • trekking
CONTACT	Desa Kedewatan, Ubud 80571 • telephone: +62.361.980 252 • facsimile: +62.361.980 253 • email: reservation@puriwulandari.net • website: www.puriwulandari.net

PHOTOGRAPHS COURTESY OF PURI WULANDARI.

Taman Bebek

Of the many beautiful hotels located throughout Bali, Taman Bebek is particularly attractive to those who seek a harmonious marriage of nature and culture within a quiet and contemplative village setting.

Taman Bebek stands on the exact site of the late American ethnomusicologist Colin McPhee's old residence. In the 1930s, the young music researcher moved to Bali to study the gamelan and returned to the United States in the 1940s to promote this traditional Indonesian musical instrument.

In the late 1970s, landscape designer Made Wijaya began work to transform the property into a stylish holiday bungalow, and over the years built extensions and annexes until its present form took shape. The first suite, built in the style of mountain Bali houses and overlooking the river, was built in 1979, while the first of the quaint

THIS PAGE: Flourishing gardens around the bungalows and pools create a sense of intimacy and seclusion.
OPPOSITE: The private entrance to one of Taman Bebek's comfortable bungalows.

and spacious colonial-style 'Queenslander' cottages was built in 1984. Three new bungalows were added six years later, done up in distinctive dark green and powder blue hues respectively. The two-bedroom Presidential Suite, a substantial house with a private pool, was completed in 1994. Built facing the valley, it is reminiscent of a tiered wantilan and has a grand Sumba-style pool deck lined with Sumba artworks. It offers more space and enhanced features, and is well-suited to wedding parties and large families. Finally, in 2000, a Malaysian Trengganu-style villa was added to the mix.

Today, Taman Bebek has six roomy bungalows with either one or two bedrooms each. The villas are all fully furnished and house many eye-catching artworks, from lovely bamboo creations to rustic, patterned textiles and exotic carvings. Particularly captivating are the carved inlays and decorative shell pieces, as well as the stone sculptures that are of great symbolic significance to the locals.

You'll find many artworks from Made Wijaya's personal collection, obtained from around the region, in the hotel's gardens as well, and they never fail to engage guests in hours of contemplative appreciation. The authentic Balinese items in particular, have been sourced from local artisans and bear their signature styles while showcasing great

attention to detail. Among the leading sculptors with works on display here are Diana Darling and Wayan Cemul from Ubud, and Dewa Oka from Ketewel. Works in a variety of other styles have also been imported to liven up the bungalows' living spaces and lend a romantic, escapist air to the hotel. In particular, many guests find the decorative interior paintwork and a series of watercolour paintings most memorable. These were produced by Australian artist Stephen Little and were inspired by the evocative train station scenes featured in the movie *Bwana Junction*. From the café to the reception area, guests will find contributions from many other international artists and designers who stopped by to share their talents.

No matter which residence guests choose, they can look forward to a grand bathroom complete with mosaic patterns and pebbles, framed by a lush garden of tropical plants. The private outdoor shower is located on the edge of the hillside and offers a rare experience as you lather up while taking in views of the Balinese countryside spread out in front of you.

The café at Taman Bebek, designed by Neville Marsh, offers hot meals throughout the day, with a menu of local delights and a choice of contemporary international cuisine. Savour your meals on the terrace

and enjoy views of the gorgeous landscape. Delectable highlights from the menu include a refreshing cucumber salad, a mountain vegetable soup, crispy fried eel cooked with fragrant Asian spices, and the traditional chicken or duck betutu. The main courses are served with rice and local delicacies.

Private dining can also be arranged in the seclusion of your bungalow. Should you decide to prepare your own food, you can do so in the bungalow's kitchenette. Alternatively, order from room service and have your meal in the dining area or on the generous verandah. If you want to head outside for dinner, just make your way into Ubud's centre and take your pick of restaurants serving food to suit all palates, before making a stop in one of the town's many trendy bars for a nightcap.

As for activities and services, there's something to suit all needs at Taman Bebek, from cooking classes, to baby-sitters, and rugged outdoor excursions or water sports for those seeking physically challenging exploits. Guests can also sign up for Taman Bebek's eye-opening tours of Ubud and the surrounding villages.

The resort's spa is in a cosy venue and offers a range of massages and beauty treatments. Its manager, Made Tabanan, is a veteran of the industry and his expert hands have left many guests feeling relaxed over the last 15 years. An hour or two spent under his care is the perfect way to bring an end to your day at Taman Bebek.

THIS PAGE (FROM LEFT): Local and foreign artists have contributed to the extensive collection at Taman Bebek; pebbled pathways lead guests around the lush property.
OPPOSITE: Covered decks offer a cosy spot at which to unwind with a good book or enjoy your afternoon tea.

FACTS

ROOMS	6 Valley View Villas • 1 Presidential Suite
FOOD	local and international
DRINK	wine bar
FEATURES	pool • spa • private art collection
NEARBY	Ubud centre • tour guides
CONTACT	Sayan, Ubud 80571 • telephone: +62.361.975 385 • facsimile: +62.361.976 532 • email: info@tamanbebek.com • website: www.tamanbebek.com

PHOTOGRAPHS COURTESY OF TAMAN BEBEK.

Uma Ubud

Uma Ubud offers comfort, culture and well-being in a complete and holistic package. It is located on the outskirts of Ubud, amidst a lush backdrop of paddy fields, coconut palms and banyan trees. With its three hectares (seven acres) of land, Uma Ubud is well positioned to enjoy a scenic overview of the Campuhan valley, distant volcanoes and the Oos river fringing it. This provides a natural buffer that keeps Uma Ubud free from the distractions provided by Ubud's many attractions lying within convenient walking distance, so that guests can enjoy the tranquil pleasures and comprehensive hospitality that the resort offers.

Uma Ubud has 29 luxurious double rooms and suites. These include 10 rooms with attached courtyards, 14 rooms with garden terraces, four suites with private lounges—three of which have infinity-edged pools—and an exclusive Shambhala Suite which comes with a private pool and a treatment area where traditional local and Asian spa therapies can be enjoyed.

The team responsible for the architecture and design of the property comprise a trio with significant experience in Bali's resort circuit: architect Cheong Yew Kwan, whose work here reflects the needs of modern resort living while remaining faithful to local traditions, interior architect Koichiro Ikebuchi, who has a keen eye for capturing and reflecting the area's natural features and cultural characteristics in minimalist style, and landscape architect Trevor Hillier,

THIS PAGE (FROM TOP): Full length glass doors open to reveal landscaped gardens; bedrooms feature simple but stylish décor.
OPPOSITE: The resort's minimalist style is best expressed in the dramatic bathrooms.

whose passion for nature has ensured that the resort's exterior is in aesthetic harmony with the surrounding landscape.

The resort's restaurant Kemiri, which means 'candlenut' locally—paying tribute to an ingredient actively used in Balinese cuisine—seats 70 guests indoors and outdoors. There is also a more exclusive dining bale available, suitable for parties of up to a dozen guests. The restaurant is situated next to a waterfall-fed pond and remains cool and breezy under a traditional thatched alang-alang roof.

The kitchen caters for meals throughout the day and specialises in contemporary interpretations of Indonesian and Sumatran cuisine in particular. There is also a strong emphasis on spicy Indian flavours. Seasonal local produce provided by nearby farms play a part in keeping the menu fresh.

Diet-conscious guests will no doubt appreciate the resort's COMO Shambhala cuisine which uses only raw, organic foods that are rich in living enzymes, vitamins and sea minerals. Processed sugar, for example, is replaced with honey, while blended nut milk is used instead of cow's milk. In this manner, guests enjoy a cleansing of their digestive systems while learning more about healthy eating and living.

The focus on well-being is enhanced by the COMO Shambhala Retreat which offers

a range of personalised treatments including Ayurvedic detoxification and therapeutic baths. The retreat has four treatment rooms, a reflexology area, an open-air yoga pavilion, a meditation bale, steam and sauna rooms, and a swimming pool.

One of the signature treatments here is the Uma Bath, which is a basic cleansing treatment that exfoliates and softens skin with a salt scrub infused with essential oils, such as macadamia and oat bran. The treatment ends with a relaxing massage.

Also on the menu is the Balinese Spice Body Mask. This treatment uses hand-crushed rice blended with black pepper, cloves, cinnamon, nutmeg and ginger to produce an effective deep-heat experience. Through a therapeutic massage at the end, guests will find their tired muscles and rheumatic tendencies soon relieved. Also a highlight is the Abhyanga, an Ayurvedic treatment that uses warm herbal oils applied in a rhythmic massage to loosen toxins in the body and boost blood circulation.

Uma Ubud has drawn upon the talents of many nutritionists and therapists to ensure that the requirements of each guest are appropriately recognised and addressed through daily routines and exercises. In fact, bodywork is a key element of the COMO Shambhala experience and a wide range of yoga sessions are available to enhance

THIS PAGE (FROM TOP): *Kemiri's open-air setting is perfect for casual meals; lily-filled ponds are scattered around the resort.*

OPPOSITE: *Though the interiors are chic and contemporary, a blend of influences, both Indonesian and Asian, can still be observed.*

guests' awareness of how physical and psychological well-being are intricately linked. To further accentuate the focus on a healthy lifestyle, the organic foods used in Kemiri's menu are also used in the resort's customised bath and bodycare products.

Uma Ubud's dedication to personal well-being extends to mental stimulation as well, with numerous tours, treks and sporting activities available to widen your cultural horizons and push you to your limit. These include tours to galleries and museums in Ubud such as the Neka Art Museum and Museum Puri Lukisan, trekking and biking through paddy fields, forests and along the banks of the Ayung, volcano climbing, and cultural excursions to nearby temples and villages to witness religious ceremonies and traditional Balinese performances such as a gamelan orchestra or Kecak fire dance.

FACTS		
ROOMS	14 Terrace Rooms • 10 Garden Rooms • 1 Uma Suite • 3 Uma Pool Suites • 1 Shambhala Suite	
FOOD	Kemiri: Indonesian and Sumatran	
DRINK	pool bar • mini-bar	
FEATURES	pool • spa • limousines • personal shopping assistants • customised tours	
BUSINESS	business centre • Internet access	
NEARBY	trekking • river rafting • Neka Art Museum • homeware and antique shops	
CONTACT	Jalan Raya Sanggingan, Banjar Lungsiakan, Kedewatan, Ubud 80571 • telephone: +62.361.972 448 • facsimile: +62.361.972 449 • email: res.ubud@uma.como.bz • website: uma.como.bz	

PHOTOGRAPHS COURTESY OF UMA UBUD.

Waka Namya

Waka Namya is located in Penestanan village, part of the artistic community of Ubud. This traditional, Balinese-style resort resembles a rice storage facility known locally as a lumbung. This means you can expect spacious interiors and high ceilings beneath thatched alang alang roofs.

The resort's 11 rooms include three spacious Lanai Rooms and eight Deluxe Villas. Both types of accommodation are suitable for families, groups of friends and couples, while its compact size ensures everyone enjoys some privacy and an overall good time. In every room, traditional Balinese aesthetics meet contemporary style and comfort. The interior features a mix of local stone, woven fabrics, bamboo and weathered wood. Every corner is tastefully accessorised with native artworks or fabrics with intriguing ethnic prints. To complement this earthy design, all rooms come with their own lush tropical garden. As with the rest of the property, every element used, every view that catches the eye, has been deliberately

THIS PAGE (CLOCKWISE FROM RIGHT): *Every room is tastefully accessorised with Balinese fabrics and artefacts; traditional Balinese touches inspire self-reflection; rooms come complete with outdoor showers and large sunken bathtubs.*
OPPOSITE: *Enjoy afternoon tea by the pool.*

employed to create an artistic yet understated setting, making it a charming addition to Ubud's cultural landscape.

Those who enjoy leisurely showers will appreciate the sumptuous sunken bathtub and the additional luxury of an outdoor shower. After such a shower, guests can slip into a sarong and laze around on the terrace, or let the handmade mosquito net curtains down and take a nap in the always-beckoning bed.

When it's time for tea, adjourn to the pool or the resort's restaurant where you'll be served ginger tea and Balinese sweets. If that doesn't fill you up, a full meal at the restaurant should. Here, you can tuck into Indonesian specialities served in a traditional Balinese setting.

Waka Namya is also home to a spa where guests can indulge in a variety of treatments using aromatic oils and exotic blends of natural ingredients. A favourite activity with guests, however, is to simply relax by the pool. Here, guests can snack on light sandwiches and enjoy refreshments.

When you feel it's time to explore the world outside Waka Namya, the resort can organise treks around the verdant rice fields. These early-morning treks, led by the resort's staff, bring guests through the intricate web of fields and onto a farmer's path to witness traditional methods of planting, irrigation and harvesting rice (this depends on the season though). River rafting on the fast-flowing Campuhan is another option.

Other tours lead guests into Ubud's cultural centre and provide an opportunity to pick up some traditional Balinese artwork and handicrafts while taking in the area's numerous sights and sounds. You're sure to leave Bali with more than a mere souvenir once you've explored Ubud.

With its handy location away from the hustle and bustle of Ubud, but near enough to fully enjoy Bali's artistic hub, Waka Namya offers guests the best of both worlds.

FACTS		
ROOMS	3 Lanai Rooms • 8 Deluxe Villas	
FOOD	restaurant: Balinese, Indonesian and Western	
DRINK	poolside bar	
FEATURES	spa • pool • trekking • river rafting • tours of Ubud	
BUSINESS	Internet access	
NEARBY	Ubud centre • Celuk • Goa Gajah • Monkey Forest • Tampaksiring	
CONTACT	Penestanan Street, Ubud 80571 • telephone: +62.361.975 719 • facsimile: +62.361.975 719 • email: wakanamya@wakaexperience.com • website: www.wakaexperience.com	

PHOTOGRAPHS COURTESY OF WAKA NAMYA.

Waka di Ume

THIS PAGE: *Enjoy a dip in a private swimming pool while verdant rice fields sway in the breeze.*

OPPOSITE (CLOCKWISE FROM LEFT): *Mosquito net curtains add to the rooms' tropical charm; each balcony or terrace overlooks the Ubud countryside; the interior features a mix of traditional Balinese and contemporary styles.*

Located in Bali's cultural centre, Ubud, Waka di Ume is a boutique resort that captures the spirit of the area with great charm. Designed and built by Ketut Siandana, and owned and operated by the Waka family, the slim and long resort sits on a strip of land along the top of a rice field. Though views of rice fields are common to the Balinese, to the visitor, such views add to the resort's exotic appeal and blend well with Waka di Ume's winning combination of traditional Balinese aesthetics and contemporary style.

The property is cosy, with 16 Lanais, villas and suites, along with a two-storey restaurant, spa, massage centre and a main pool. Waka di Ume's modest size is, however, one of its main selling points as guests are assured of privacy and a real sense of being in a retreat.

Nowhere is this more apparent than in the resort's loft-like meditation room which is located on the top floor of the massage centre at one end of the scenic property. This room overlooks the split-level cascade swimming pool and inspires quietude and reflection. Take the time to indulge in some spa treatments which make the most of Indonesian herbs and spices.

The range of available lodging consists of 11 Lanais, four suites and one villa. Besides the quintessential Waka features such as a sunken bath and beds with intricate mosquito net curtains, each room has its own terrace or balcony with unobstructed views. The double-storey suites are the most spacious, of course, and can accommodate up to four guests each. Three of these suites—Waka, Premium Palm and Palm—come with private pools as well. The resort's only villa is slightly

smaller, while the Lanai rooms are best suited to single or double occupancy.

Dining is not forgotten at Wake di Ume. The restaurant in the main building offers guests two different dining experiences, with Western-style seating on the lower level, and a more traditional arrangement of floor pillows and low tables upstairs. This is a cosy spot at which to sample the Balinese fare whipped up by the talented kitchen crew while taking in the view.

For recreational activities outside the resort, sign up for Waka di Ume's land tours and trekking expeditions. These informative activities will introduce you to the many wonders of Ubud's lush countryside.

FACTS	**ROOMS**	11 Lanai Suites • 1 Papaya Villa • 1 Premium Palm Suite • 1 Terrace Suite • 1 Palm Suite • 1 Waka Suite
	FOOD	restaurant: Balinese, Indonesian and Western
	DRINK	mini-bar
	FEATURES	pool • trekking • meditation room • land tours
	BUSINESS	IDD telephone
	NEARBY	Ubud centre • Monkey Forest • White Heron Village • Goa Gajah
	CONTACT	Jalan Sueta, Ubud 80571 • telephone: +62.361.973 178 • facsimile: +62.361.973 179 • email: wakadiume@wakaexperience.com • website: www.wakaexperience.com

PHOTOGRAPHS COURTESY OF WAKA DI UME.

Kirana Spa

With spa holidays growing in popularity, travellers are expecting more and more from their chosen spa resort, and this has led to an improvement in the quality of such destinations in terms of services, staff and accommodation. One establishment that has been drawing the weary and stressed with its spa-focused luxury is Kirana Spa.

Located in the verdant hills of Ubud, Kirana Spa extends over 18,000 sq m (21,528 sq yd) along the Ayung River valley. Inspired by its grand surroundings, the spa is dedicated to bringing about a return to a natural state of being, where guests are utterly relaxed and at peace with themselves. The spa takes its name from the ancient Sanskrit word 'kirana', which means 'light' or 'aura'. In its more contemporary usage in Bahasa Indonesia, it refers to inner beauty, transcending physical attributes.

The spa's visual appeal is the result of a collaboration between architect Lek Bunnag, whose academic circuit includes Harvard University, the National University of Singapore and Hong Kong University, and his professional partner Bill Bensley,

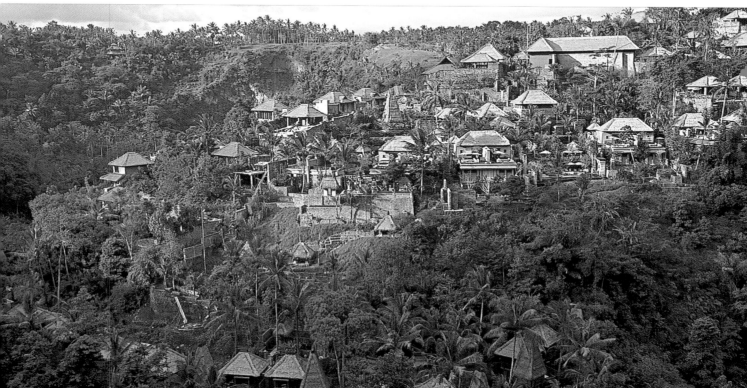

...dedicated to bringing about a return to a natural state of being...

THIS PAGE (CLOCKWISE FROM LEFT):
A vibrant path leads the way to one of eight Treatment Villas; a private jacuzzi in the Suite Villa offers picturesque views; sculptures inspired by local mythology dot the expansive propety.
OPPOSITE: Stone walkways and a hillside setting give Kirana Spa a village-like atmosphere.

a landscape architect who has supervised many high-profile projects around Asia.

Kirana Spa follows the Zen-influenced concept of 'nullity', where it is believed individuals need to return to a 'zero' state before the ability to experience even the simplest joy can be realised. Thus, the spa's commitment to highlighting the powerful healing benefits that are available in the natural landscape all around, has drawn a stream of guests from all over the world, eager to experience some true downtime.

Entirely luxurious and relaxing, the villas here provide an ideal setting to experience the spa's treatments in comfort and luxury. Guests can choose from the Treatment Villas, Suite Villas or the Presidential Villa, all of which include their own treatment, shower and dressing rooms. The Presidential Villa features both a hot and cold jacuzzi, a relaxation arbor and a private plunge pool on its upper level. The lower level is just as well-equipped, with both a normal sauna and a herbal mist sauna. The Suite Villas offer the same amenities in a slightly smaller setting, but do not include a cold jacuzzi or a relaxation arbor. Instead, a luxurious day bed is available for your pleasure. The Treatment Villas come with the essentials like treatment, shower and dressing rooms.

There are two types of spa programmes available—the Private Spa Programme, which offers a combination of Treatment Time and Spa Time, and the Spa Treatment

programme, which consists solely of a series of treatments. These allow guests to spend as much or as little time as they want enjoying treatments and Kirana's facilities. The Private Spa Programme can be experienced in both the Suite Villas and Presidential Villa. Guests can choose from a three-hour, half-day or one-day programme that includes a combination of Treatment Time and Spa Time. The one-day package includes a light meal. If you're staying in the Presidential Villa, you can also indulge in a full-day exclusive programme. Over at the Treatment Villas, guests can choose between 120-minute or 60-minute treatments from an extensive menu that includes massages, foot and leg treatments, facials and more.

Whatever programme you opt for, you'll be allowed access to Kirana's lovely Spa Garden—a fascinating area with water features, overflowing with tropical foliage. Here, guests are free to frolic in two pools, relax in a jacuzzi or sauna, or just laze around. This is where guests should head to right after receiving a treatment, to relax and quietly revel in the solitude.

The treatments at Kirana Spa are based on original systems and techniques that have

THIS PAGE (CLOCKWISE FROM RIGHT):
The Spa Garden is a sanctuary for guests who need to unwind; treatment rooms in the Suite Villas offer a view of the private plunge pool; cosy corners to relax in abound at Kirana Spa.

OPPOSITE: Enjoy some quiet time in a pavilion.

been cultivated for over a century. These combine the artful application of treatments through skilful pressure from sensitive and warm hands, to bring about blissful relaxation and a deep awakening. Foremost among Kirana's treatments are the arts of Shoku and Atsu, which rely on touch and pressure to alleviate tension and stiffness while channelling energy through the body. The Rhythm of Respiration treatment aids a deeper and longer breathing rhythm by harmonising your respiratory instincts with the relaxing and intoxicating environment around you. Likewise, the Tokumyaku and Ninmyaku treatments seek to redirect the flow of Qi, or internal energy, in a manner that optimises the balance between the physical and the mental, thus channelling energy throughout your body.

With their winning combination of warm smiles, skilful hands, state-of-the-art facilities and sincere hospitality, Kirana Spa will definitely surpass your expectations.

FACTS

TREATMENTS	facials • massages • foot and leg therapy
FOOD	delivered from restaurants in Ubud
DRINK	mini-bar • Spa Garden
FEATURES	pool • spa • jacuzzi • sauna • private treatment villas • unique massage methods developed by Shiseido
NEARBY	Ubud market • Ayung River valley
CONTACT	Desa Kedewatan, Ubud 80571 • telephone: +62.361.976 333 • facsimile: +62.361.974 888 • email: info-english@kiranaspa.com • website: www.kiranaspa.com

PHOTOGRAPHS COURTESY OF KIRANA SPA.

Spa at Ibah Luxury Villas

Spa at Ibah Luxury Villas is operated by Mandara Spa and has been consistently earning accolades for its gracious staff and memorable service. The spa is located in a villa within the grounds of Ibah Luxury Villas and provides an experience that some say might be best appreciated when travelling alone, so as to heighten the meditative intensity and allow for some much-needed quality time with yourself.

Balinese therapies are practised well here and exotic spa treatments are applied with expert consideration. The many frowns, cares and worries caused by urban life are massaged and coaxed into oblivion as the body unwinds and unknots within private treatment rooms that feature a pleasing décor marrying reassuring beams of timber with long, flowing fabrics. The impressive jacuzzi is positioned to allow an unhurried survey of the verdant hills all around, and provides a most inspiring way to spend a lazy afternoon.

Guests are invited to mark the start of their stay with an introductory spa treatment, and the intoxicating experience is often immediately addictive. Whether it is the weariness of jet lag, or the strain of daily life, the strength of the slow but sure relief afforded by a massage here will lift your spirits. The treatments are focused on the body, the face and the senses. In the hands of the spa's experienced therapists, simple Balinese treatments will very quickly soothe your body and improve blood circulation while calming nervous impulses as well.

A signature treatment here is the Mandara Massage, a session that combines aspects of Shiatsu, Thai, Hawaiian Lomi Lomi, Swedish and Balinese massage styles applied by a pair of therapists working together. Unique aromatherapy oils created specially by the spa enhance the experience of this original treatment. Guests can choose from four exotic oils: Mandara, a sensual

THIS PAGE: The spa's jacuzzi overlooks the lush Campuhan valley in Ubud's countryside.

OPPOSITE: Long, draping curtains in neutral colours contrast with dark wood furnishings.

combination of sandalwood, ylang ylang, patchouli and cananga oils; Island Spice, an aromatic blend of spices including clove, ginger and nutmeg; Harmony, a citrous mix of mandarin, lavender, bergamot and ylang ylang; and Tranquillity, a fusion of lavender, vertiver, ylang ylang and cananga.

The Traditional Facial, another signature treatment, uses Indonesian herbs and spices, tropical fruits and vegetables in age-old beauty recipes to cleanse and leave your skin looking and feeling radiant. A neck, shoulder, hand and foot massage round off this enticing treatment.

Those after some private time here will delight in the deluxe Spa Villa that comes with an indoor massage suite and jacuzzi. This is where guests should indulge in a traditional Indonesian body scrub like the Bali Kopi or coconut scrubs.

In short, a visit to this spa will leave you feeling calm and relaxed as you leave to explore Bali's many attractions.

FACTS

TREATMENTS	massages • body scrubs • facials
FOOD	The Restaurant and Bar: Indonesian and Asian
DRINK	Tembako Cigar and Whiskey Lounge
FEATURES	Spa Villa • jacuzzi • unique aromatherapy oils
NEARBY	Ubud centre • Gunung Lebah • holy springs
CONTACT	Tjampuhan, Ubud 80571 • telephone: +62.361.974 466 • facsimile: +62.361.974 467 • email: ibah@dps.centrin.net.id • website: www.ibahbali.com

PHOTOGRAPHS COURTESY OF SPA AT IBAH LUXURY VILLAS.

Ary's Warung

It's easy to find your way to Ary's Warung since it occupies one of the most central and lively spots along the main road. Many come from far and wide to dine on the cool terrace of Ubud's renowned restaurant, enjoy the tantalising food offered and take obligatory snapshots at the nearby temples.

Indeed, there is nothing at all average about an evening at Ary's Warung. Considering the many Balinese dining options available around the island, Ary's Warung is not for the feeble or undiscerning. It very strongly establishes its position as a leading restaurant with an uncompromising dedication to providing a truly memorable dining experience marked by quality and style. This is immediately obvious in the lower level which is occupied by a lavish lounge that is reminiscent of similarly refined spots in cosmopolitan cities around the world. Wine and cigars are the order of the day in this chic retreat. The lounge is perfect for occasional luncheons and cocktail receptions, and hints at the type of guest who will feel right at home here. The broad dining area on the upper floor includes an open verandah which benefits from the breeze that wafts by regularly.

Since its inception in 1986, Ary's Warung has been consistently drawing the crowds with its evolving and innovative menu. In fact, guests will find decision-making quite a challenge as the bold range of options calls for a little bit of everything.

THIS PAGE: Located in the centre of town, Ary's classy bar is the perfect spot to unwind with one of their cool Martinis.

OPPOSITE: Ubud's more discerning bar-hoppers readily call these seats home.

For this very reason, both the lunch and dinner menus comprise a four- and six-course tasting menu respectively, served in modest portions so that you're free to enjoy a more varied encounter with the restaurant's signature tastes and flavours; though single dishes may be requested if any are particularly preferred.

A typical dining experience could include the full-bodied Vegetable Soup, presented hot or chilled, followed by a dish of succulent Lobster Wontons or Coconut King Prawns served with sweet corn, black beans and avocado. Then, you can expect a pleasant change in taste and tempo as a plate of classic Seared Sea Scallops accompanied by juicy asparagus and green beans is presented, or a delightful serving of Steamed Zucchini Flowers with seafood and a pomelo salad arrive at your table.

The kitchen unfailingly lives up to its promise of only serving catch while it is still firm and fresh, and employs condiments largely to enhance the original flavour instead of overpowering it. Ary's Warung prides itself on the use of fresh, organic ingredients and choice meats, combined with inspired yet unpretentious preparation.

One of many popular dishes here is the Pork Belly Babi Guling in Ibu Oka spices, served with young coconut and banana flower lawar. A spiced baked apple rounds

off this succulent dish. Another favourite is the Rack of Lamb served with a clever combination of chilli mint sauce and a sweet potato rosti. Also high on the list are the Roasted Veal Cutlets that come drizzled with just a touch of tangy wasabi butter.

The Grilled Salmon served with spinach gnocchi and a kaffir lime leaf broth, and the Slow-Roasted Ubud Duck Betutu served with blanched fern tips in a plecing sauce and poached tamarelo, are as mouth-watering as they are joltingly creative.

For those who believe that the best things in life come right after dinner, Ary's has a dessert menu that will leave those with a sweet tooth dizzy with joy. If you have an experimental palate, then the best of this selection is the Durian Brûlée, which has warmed the heart of a jaded food critic or two. The citrus toppings provide a refreshing contrast to the aromatic and strong flavour of the durian, while the toffee adds a sweet note. In a similar manner, the rich Chocolate Ginger Kahlua Cream Tart teases with a satisfying Kahlua rush. There's also the likes of the Coconut Custard Pie, Fresh Mixed Berries with Champagne Jellies, and the Rhubarb and Marscapone Cheese Tart to choose from. These creative indulgences will please your palate and have you wondering about the culinary geniuses who came up with these intoxicating combinations.

THIS PAGE (CLOCKWISE FROM RIGHT):
Savour acclaimed wines at the stylish lounge; intriguing Balinese design details liven up Ary's minimalist interior; ascend the stairway to an exquisite dining experience on Ary's second level.

OPPOSITE (CLOCKWISE FROM LEFT):
Nothing less than the best is served at these tables; Ary's hors d'oeuvres taste as good as they look; do try the Tuna Parfait served with caviar and wasabi cream.

As might be expected, the wine list does not disappoint either and serves to complement the menu as far as possible. Ary's Warung has a wine cellar carrying about 160 noteworthy labels from around the world, with an emphasis on French and Australian wines. A selection of cocktails and Balinese beverages also promise to add a little kick to your dining experience.

This restaurant has a positively upmarket vibe and no matter when you choose to turn up, there's bound to be an exciting mix of people from all over the world present, either enjoying a romantic dinner, catching up with friends and family or simply having a couple of drinks before venturing out into Ubud's buzzing nightlife. In short, this is a centre for sophisticated wining and dining, and it is also quite clearly a leading light in Ubud's dining scene; indeed, nothing less should be expected of Ary's Warung.

FACTS

SEATS	terrace: 96 • lounge: 62
FOOD	contemporary Balinese-Asian
DRINK	bar • lounge • wine cellar
FEATURES	innovative tasting menu • cigar lounge
NEARBY	Ubud centre and market • village temple • water garden temple
CONTACT	Jalan Raya Ubud, Ubud 80571 • telephone: +62.361.975 053 • fax: +62.361.978 359 • email: aryswarung@dekco.com • website: www.dekco.com

PHOTOGRAPHS COURTESY OF ARY'S WARUNG.

Kedai

THIS PAGE: *Kedai's casual setting makes it a popular spot with holiday-makers.*

OPPOSITE (CLOCKWISE FROM LEFT): *Experience a sunset in Bali while enjoying a meal by the beach; indulge in a traditional Indonesian dessert of deep-fried bananas with dark chocolate and cheddar cheese; the tasty crab cakes are a favourite with diners.*

Visitors to picturesque east Bali and the seaside town of Candidasa will have a lot more to take in than the history, culture and physical beauty of the region; they will also find themselves drawn to a lovely little restaurant along the beach. Rustic and elegant, the bamboo-and-thatch structure that is Kedai hints at the rich legacy of historical Bali by merging aspects of Balinese design and the Lombok-style Sasak house with a depth of authenticity that rewards guests who take the time to scrutinise and appreciate it.

With its uncut, thatched alang alang roof and open setting, Kedai offers guests a relaxed dining experience complemented by stunning sea views. As open and breezy as the place is, however, it also offers privacy with an interior designed to incorporate intimate clusters. This ensures each dinner party is enclosed within its own little world. The restaurant's in-house hospitality guidelines nurture this further, as groups are generally seated with no more than six to eight guests at a table.

To match the stand-out exterior, Kedai's menu shows great respect for the culinary styles of Indonesia, and Bali in particular, while exploring new horizons with contemporary Asian cuisine. The chefs have designed the menu to accommodate the daily arrivals of local fish and other seafood, which are cooked following various Asian styles, but prepared and presented in a Western manner. The emphasis is on fresh seafood as a result, with tastes ranging from spicy to sweet and savoury.

The wide and mouth-watering menu features standard fare like crab cakes, curries and mixed-grill satay, along with highly recommended dishes like the Spicy Calamari Salad, Grilled Fresh Catch of the

...each dinner party is enclosed within its own little world.

Day and the tantalising Seafood Spring Roll Sticks. Although there is only one menu for lunch and dinner, daily and weekly specials will keep you coming back for more.

Vegatarians have not been forgotten either. Kedai has a number of dishes created specially for vegetarians, and the chefs have put as much effort into preparing such tempting options like the Mixed Vegetable Laksa and Vegatarian Homemade Spicy Curry as they have with any other dish on the menu. To add to the restaurant's appeal, only organic produce is used.

Though Candidasa has numerous restaurants eager to please your palate with their specialities, Kedai remains a leader because of its constantly evolving menu, and its dedication to creativity and quality.

FACTS		
	SEATS	44
	FOOD	contemporary Balinese-Asian seafood
	DRINK	extensive wine list
	FEATURES	Lombok-style Sasak architecture • organic produce • vegetarian options • beachfront venue
	NEARBY	Candidasa centre • beach
	CONTACT	Jalan Raya Candidasa, Candidasa, Karangasem 80851 • telephone: +62.363.420 20 • facsimile: +62.361.420 18 • email: kedai@dekco.com • website: www.dekco.com

PHOTOGRAPHS COURTESY OF KEDAI.

Lamak Restaurant + Bar

With its intriguing display of twisted rails, suggestive swirls and surreal jungle elements, the funky and youthful vibe of Lamak Restaurant and Bar is immediately obvious. But that is not to say that it doesn't mean serious business when it comes to food. If anything, Lamak has enlivened Bali's dining scene with its unpretentious originality which appeals to both locals and tourists. The restaurant's pronounced eclecticism, proven by its menu and design, is not out of place either, given the proximity of Ubud's artistic district.

Located along Monkey Forest Road and occupying a prominent spot in front of Cendana Hotel, Lamak is rendered even more arresting with a building designed by award-winning landscape artist Made Wijaya. Different colours, textures and images, expressed through the use of wood, stone and rich textiles, are juxtaposed energetically and enhanced with captivating shapes and outlines that give the place a very dramatic atmosphere. In Balinese culture, the use of a variety of colours reflects a reverence for the sheer diversity of the natural and spiritual world. This visual intensity is expressed all around the restaurant, from the red brick walls, to the upholstery, the cutlery and all the little details found on the furnishings and accessories.

Dramatic steel sculptures by Pintor Sirait accentuate Lamak's unique look. Especially noteworthy are the touches made to the

THIS PAGE (FROM TOP): Simple but stylish table settings; designed by Made Wijaya, Lamak is a visual treat that suits artistic Ubud perfectly. OPPOSITE: Choose to dine al fresco on the ground level or head upstairs for a lounge setting.

washrooms. Heavy steel doors have been fitted with lights—red for occupied, green for available—and the steel sinks feature water spouts that hang from the ceiling.

Managed by Roland Lickert, Lamak seats 110 patrons in open-air dining areas, an air-conditioned lounge on the second floor, and in various cosy corners.

The kitchen specialises in innovative Asian and Western cuisine, with a touch of fusion as well. Barbecued seafood and vegetarian dishes can also be expected here. There is a light lunch menu to allay the midday hunger pangs, and a long, indulgent dinner menu to turn the evening into a most memorable culinary encounter. Lamak's Executive Chef Ifah Rusdianwati is recognised for her instinctive ability to balance the authentic flavours of a particular cuisine with the introduction of unexpected tropical ingredients or foreign preparation techniques. In doing so, she produces exceptional dishes that live up to the daring attitude of the restaurant. Consider the Crab Meat Won Tons with young coconut, lime and fresh mint, the Citrus Marinated Shrimp with palm hearts and avocado slices, and the Curried Yoghurt Coated Smoked Butter Fish Medallion, which are popular with Lamak's discerning clientele.

The restaurant's penchant for updating traditional dishes shines through in their

Rijstaffel menus especially—the customary Indonesian spread of dishes served with rice. One such menu offers Tahu Petis with Sambal Pecel (fried soya bean curd with sauce and sweet peanuts) and Empek Empek Tenggiri (fish patties with palm sugar sauce) for starters, alongside the Ares Bebek (clear duck soup with banana marrow). The main course includes Gurame Goreng (crispy gurame fish with lalapan and chilli sauce) and Cumi Bakar Bumbu Sambal Tomat (grilled squid brushed with tomato chilli paste). As for dessert, tuck into a traditional Indonesian dessert, Wajik Ketan Hitam (black sticky rice cake).

With such an eclectic and extensive menu, rest assured Lamak has a beverage list to complement whatever you order. The distinctive bar has a look that is almost tribal. It sits beneath a thatched-roof pavilion with two bean-shaped, yellow-lined, mirrored shelves holding a colourful array of drink bottles. Here, diners can order a dizzying variety of spirits and liqueurs, and delicious mocktails and cocktails including the Papaya Colada, a variation of the Pina Colada, and the Markisa, a refreshing blend of vodka, pineapple liqueur, Blue Curaçao, pineapple juice, orange and passion fruit. Lamak's wine cellar, on the other hand, offers 65 labels from Australia, New Zealand, South Africa, Spain,

...the 'lamak' is an intricate religious offering made from palm leaves.

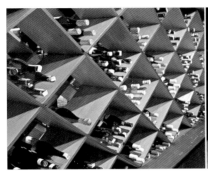

Chile, Italy, California and France. Those who enjoy a good cigar after dinner will appreciate the range available here as well.

Should you find yourself completely taken with the restaurant, you may decide to come back and hold a birthday party or similarly significant event here, and Lamak is capable of organising everything down to the smallest detail. Groups of two to 136 guests can be easily accommodated.

In its original form, the 'lamak' is an intricate religious offering made from palm leaves. Each one requires an incredible degree of skill and dedication to produce. The hectic rush of modern life has made it increasingly difficult for anyone to commit to upholding such culturally significant skills, but at Lamak Restaurant, you will observe a lingering tribute to this legacy. There are numerous lamaks of all shapes and sizes hanging tastefully inside, while certain chairs and accessories feature similar designs.

With its upbeat mix of traditional forms and contemporary style Lamak Restaurant and Bar brings Balinese culture closer to its many appreciative guests.

THIS PAGE (FROM LEFT): The walk-in wine cellar is well-stocked with imports from the Old and New Worlds; Lamak's speciality cocktails; creative murals complement the fine dining experience here.
OPPOSITE: Lamak's tribal themed bar is marked by its use of vibrant colours.

FACTS

SEATS	110
FOOD	innovative Asian and Western • fusion
DRINK	wine cellar • bar
FEATURES	weekly chef's specials • distinctive design • vegetarian menu • cigars
NEARBY	Museum Puri Lukisan • Monkey Forest
CONTACT	Jalan Monkey Forest, Ubud 80571 • telephone: +62.361.974 668 • facsimile: +62.361.973 482 • email: ptlamak@indosat.net.id • website: www.lamakbali.com

PHOTOGRAPHS COURTESY OF LAMAK RESTAURANT AND BAR.

Toko Antique

The loose conglomeration of museums, artist studios and art galleries in the Ubud area have earned this destination a lively reputation with culture-seekers. Even the more modestly entrepreneurial art collectors are known to routinely fund their Bali sojourn by picking up a few local pieces (paintings, carvings, sculptures or batik) here at a bargain and selling them for a significant profit when they return home.

Antique shoppers with a discerning and sophisticated eye recognise Ubud as a collector's hub too. It is a haven where must-have indigenous arts and crafts can be found hawked along the streets and at sidewalk stalls. For the avid collector visiting Bali for the first time though, negotiating a path through the sheer range of potential acquisitions can prove overwhelming. This is where a gallery like Toko Antique, located along Ubud's main street, comes into play.

Launched in August 2003, this new addition to the arts scene—run by the same group who gave us Treasures and Toko

THIS PAGE: Indonesian masks, vases and an array of exotic accessories are sure to catch your eye.
OPPOSITE: Stone statues like this showcase Indonesia's rich historical and cultural legacy.

...housing a wide collection of artwork from Indonesia's various regions and historical eras.

East—is an informative and spacious gallery housing a wide collection of artwork from Indonesia's various regions and historical eras. Indeed, drop by at any time and you'll find that the general quality of available pieces remains impressive, and the array of stone, wood and terracotta statues, Chinese Indonesian ceramics, textiles, antique puppets, teak products, architectural remnants, lacquerware and many other items make for a thoroughly engrossing and educational browse.

The artworks on sale are often tagged with helpful notes on their background (regional origins, material and age/period) along with other useful information. To further assist buyers, whether you're a millionaire, new to the Indonesian arts scene, looking for something to dress up your home, or simply souvenir hunting, Toko Antique can advise you on a selection of choices that best suit your needs. All you have to do is let their staff know what you would like.

Of particular interest are the intricately woven fabrics and textiles from around the Indonesian archipelago which would make perfect wall features, and the traditional masks and puppets that will surely add a little colour to your living room.

Other highlights include ceremonial objects such as holy water containers with repoussé designs featuring local motifs, tools and accessories from life in ancient Indonesia including bronze and stone oil lamps, carved axes, rice plow handles, and jewellery such as gold hair combs, hair pins, belt buckles and more.

Unlike some of the less established bargain outposts in the area, Toko Antique handles air and land deliveries with reassuring professionalism. This is indeed a point of convenience holiday-makers will whole-heartedly appreciate. Feel free to make your purchases safe in the knowledge that you will in fact see them taking a place of honour in your home.

FACTS

PRODUCTS	Indonesian antiques, artworks and artefacts • textiles • jewellery • lacquerware • masks • puppets • stoneware • woodwork
FEATURES	overseas delivery
NEARBY	Ubud centre • restaurants • cafés
CONTACT	Jalan Raya Ubud, Ubud 80571 • telephone: +62.361.975 979 • facsimile: +62.361.978 359 • email: tokoantique@dekco.com • website: www.dekco.com

PHOTOGRAPHS COURTESY OF TOKO ANTIQUE.

Toko East

Leaving your holiday destination with some quality mementos is something almost every tourist aims to achieve. In Bali, visitors head to Ubud to find the finest antiques, textiles, jewellery and art on the island. With that in mind, step into the stylish Toko East, located along Ubud's main street. Here, you'll find an array of contemporary Asian accessories and furnishings for the modern home or office.

Toko East's ('toko' translates to 'shop' in Bahasa Indonesia) slick and contemporary design contrasts with the ornate and traditional look of Pura Desa, one of Ubud's main temples, located across the bustling street. Its simple interior is best described as modern Asian, with smooth, off-white walls emphasising the spacious arrangements of the shop's wares which are displayed on unadorned glass shelves. This makes the various product categories and their respective wares instantly visible.

Feast your eyes on a range of smooth stoneware, Majapahit-inspired bronze accessories, stunning hand-blown glass, ceramics, garden and indoor lighting, intricate woodwork, silverware, seashell lacquerware and other decoratives, and

THIS PAGE (CLOCKWISE FROM RIGHT): The bronze accessories at Toko East are a popular choice with customers; serving spoons from the seashell range add a luxe touch to dinner parties; rattan balls form a lovely centrepiece.

OPPOSITE: The hand-blown glassware makes a worthy addition to any living room.

...an array of contemporary Asian accessories and furnishings...

you will definitely find yourself imagining those same items livening up your rooms and gardens back home.

Especially delightful to those who shop here is the array of table-top and corner ornaments that provide ethereal points of interest when entertaining at home. These include the charming seashell range of serving dishes and utensils, available with matching napkin rings, or the delicately woven water lily range of containers. These unusual items will surely be cause for conversation at your next dinner party.

For senior executives or home-office types with an eye for distinction, Toko East's selection of table and standing lamps will make novel additions to any office, while the teak decoratives that are artfully finished with sterling silver exude strength, determination and longevity. An extensive range of tasteful leather accessories for the office rounds off this brilliant collection.

The main strength and attraction of Toko East is its simple but elegant product range and its focus on quality products supplied by talented local designers such as Jean-

Francois, Jenggala, Seiki and Wijaya Classics and Interiors. Even at a glance, the impressive degree of master craftsmanship is clear. Under the watchful eye of manager Tara Murff, who has a string of successful art and lifestyle outlets under her belt, Toko East continues to commission only the best from the local design scene.

So when you're next in Bali, be sure to check out its cultural heart, Ubud, and Toko East in particular, for that special gift for a loved one, or that purchase which will add the finishing touch to your home or office.

FACTS

PRODUCTS Asian-inspired interior and exterior furnishings: stoneware, ceramics, hand-blown glass, teak products, lacquerware and lighting

FEATURES locally designed products

NEARBY Ubud centre • Pura Desa • restaurants • cafés

CONTACT Jalan Raya Ubud, Ubud 80571 • telephone: +62.361.978 306 • facsimile: +62.361.978 359 • email: tokoeast@dekco.com

PHOTOGRAPHS COURTESY OF TOKO EAST.

Treasures

Treasures specialises in a collection of exquisite handmade jewellery, all of which feature intricate designs that are rich in cultural significance, expertly created from 18–22K gold. What makes this store stand out from the rest is its marriage of traditional Balinese goldsmith techniques with the artistic visions and talents of a select group of like-minded designers.

This dynamic collaboration works well since the old practices of crafting jewellery tended to place a heavy emphasis on breaking new ground through innovative techniques, the materials used, the objects represented and the moods or subject matter addressed. The result is a wide range of original and one-of-a-kind jewellery that is as much a work of art as it is an accessory.

The collection at Treasures, though creatively unique in style and personality, finds common ground in influences such as nature, mythology, the animal kingdom, tribal symbolism and ancient cultures. These modes of inspiration eventually materialise in the shape of wearable and distinct jewellery made with raw gold or fine silver and set with precious or semi-precious stones. A wide variety of gems are used and many retain natural characteristics that are best described as captivatingly brazen and earthy. They are tastefully balanced with delicate metalwork and intricate designs.

Carolyn Tyler, one of Treasures' talented in-house designers, enjoys using antiquated goldsmith techniques such as granulation, filigree and repoussé to give her creations a look which is evocative of eras long gone. She prefers using 'offbeat' gems rather than flawless stones as she believes that gems, like people, gain their character, or 'spirit', through their imperfections.

Fellow in-house designer Penny Berton is dedicated to celebrating femininity. Her fascination with the representation of pagan goddesses inspired the Gifts of the Goddess collection. This stunning range of jewellery brings together ancient Chinese, Balinese and Western mythologies which have found expression in a number of innovative styles.

A third designer, Jean-Francois, breathes new life into the ancient practice of body adornment with his unique collection of tribal-inspired jewellery. He artfully combines unusual and often asymmetrical elements of diverse origins to create unique pieces.

Two new designers to check out are Tricia Kim and Lyn Fenwick. Tricia's designs are a blend of Eastern and Western styles, while Lyn focuses on classic designs which use tourmalines and Indonesian pearls.

THIS PAGE: Wearable art like these dress up even the simplest of outfits.

OPPOSITE: Treasures' stylised look is matched by a range of jewellery that gives traditional forms a contemporary update.

FACTS

PRODUCTS	innovative handmade designer jewellery using precious and semi-precious stones
FEATURES	certified products • international delivery • in-house designers • varied collections
NEARBY	Ubud centre • restaurants • cafés
CONTACT	Jalan Raya Ubud, Ubud 80571 • telephone: +62.361.976 697 • facsimile: +62.361.978 359 • email: treasures@dekco.com • website: www.treasures.dekco.com

PHOTOGRAPHS COURTESY OF TREASURES.

south+westbali

Bali Sea

Buleleng

Bangli

Karangasem

Tabanan

Gianyar

Klungkung

Indian Ocean

Lombok Strait

> The Avatara

> Waka Gangga

Badung

Badung Strait

> PT Warisan

> Hotel Tugu Bali

> Khaima Restaurant

> The Club at The Legian

> Hu'u Bar

> The Legian

> Kafe Warisan

> Ku Dé Ta

> Warisan Gallery

> The Oberoi, Bali

> Haveli

> Sienna Villas

> The Villas Bali Hotel + Spa

> Bali Niksoma

> Uluwatu Handmade Balinese Lace

> Jenggala Keramik Bali

> Villa Balquisse

> Henna Spa at Villa Balquisse

> The Istana

> Tirtha Uluwatu

Klungkung

south bali basics

South Bali, which encompasses (in a clockwise fashion) the communities of Sanur, Benoa, Nusa Dua, Bukit Jimbaran, Jimbaran Bay, Kuta, Legian, Seminyak, Canggu and Denpasar, is far and away the most populous and busy region of Bali. Most of the island's hotels, restaurants, bars, shops and beaches are concentrated here, and fine dining abounds. Despite all of this going on in such a small space, somehow the atmosphere is still relaxed, fresh and totally irresistible.

South Bali boasts the island's biggest city, the busiest beaches, the most vibrant nightlife, the most chill-out lounges, the best surf, the most luxurious spas, and heaps of style to burn. It has a lot going on, but the laid-back vibe of Bali still resounds beneath it all, so you can always find an oasis of peace in the gardens, on the beaches, or poolside at one of its villas, spas or resorts.

luxe living and loud surf: nusa dua and environs

There is a doorknob-shaped peninsula dangling off the lower edge of Bali called Nusa Dua, meaning 'second island'. It is a hilly region of limestone surrounded by cliffs dropping into the sea. Because the area is quite dry, it was never used for agriculture, and so Nusa Dua was left relatively untouched.

In the 1970s, the Indonesian government recognised the potential of international tourism and decided to develop Nusa Dua into a world-class resort area, inviting investors and major players in the travel industry to participate. The result was a carefully planned constellation of five-star luxury resorts, a championship golf course, and retail and restaurant space. Immediately bordering Nusa Dua are, to the northeast, Tanjung Benoa, and to the northwest, Bukit Jimbaran and Jimbaran Bay. These districts have the same flavour as the main Nusa Dua development itself: they offer full-service resorts with all the trimmings, from court sports to water sports and activities for the kids.

Lately, astute hoteliers and investors have been creating villa complexes of stunning beauty in Nusa Dua, often with dramatic views and good access to excellent beaches.

PAGE 108: The surf breaks are clean and reliable at the beaches near Uluwatu, which means great rides for surfers and superb views for sunbathers.

THIS PAGE: Sanur is a paradise for water sports enthusiasts.

OPPOSITE: The almost deserted beach at Canggu is a haven for those who want some quiet time.

Particularly in the neighbourhood of Bukit Jimbaran, stretching down to Jimbaran Bay, one finds a kind of dignified, classic luxury. The bay itself has a beautiful beach with dozens of open-air, grilled fish cafés. No visit here would be the same without enjoying a meal at one of these casual outdoor settings.

The cliffs along the northwest coast of Nusa Dua drop down steeply to a series of fantastic surf beaches that are household names among the world's wave riders. These beaches are not just for surfers either. In recent years they have developed their own beach scene and have become daytime destinations for the young and in-the-know. Most popular among them are Dreamland and Balangan beaches, where you can rent a beach chair and umbrella, and lie back to soak up the sun while watching world-class surfers ride the waves. It is a very relaxed scene and many expatriates come for the day to escape the more touristy beaches, mingling with young Europeans on holiday and eager surfers from all over the world. These are beaches where you are likely to see more skin than swimsuit.

kooky kulture: kuta and legian

The tourist heartlands of Kuta and Legian consist of one main road and a bewildering network of narrow lanes, plus a beachside strip, all of them bursting with shops, street vendors, cafés, pubs and bungalows. Flashy shopfronts vie for your attention, DVD sellers abound, and batik sarongs, cold drinks, bikinis, souvenirs and surfboards are offered everywhere you turn. It is a young, fun and wacky world, and you can find some very interesting places to nip into down Kuta's little lanes. The beach is big and brash, and often very busy, with a strong flavour of California and Australia blended with just a little bit of Coney Island.

the villa-fied life of seminyak and beyond

Hip expatriates and tropical entrepreneurs inhabit the zone that stretches from Legian to Canggu. They tend to be more beach and bar focused, and are here for the lifestyle, not just the luxury. The area is Kuta all grown-up, but equally fun in its own way.

The beach along the Seminyak stretch is more exclusive and less developed than the beaches further south. It is quieter, more suited to a peaceful walk, and lined with an assortment of expensive villas and elegant resorts.

Just a little inland, you'll discover a number of villas hidden away along small lanes. There are villas for sale, and for rent by the day, week or month, and there's something to suit different styles and budgets. The villa lifestyle is focused on being socially active and psychologically attuned to where you are. It is about truly being and staying, not just passing through this tropical island.

Seminyak is Bali's capital of chic, and it is extremely international. It is also the centre of creative entrepreneurism, with oodles of clever, collaborative businesses run by expatriates and locals sprouting up every year. They produce and market all kinds of innovative things through their cottage industries, from fashion and footwear, to furniture and stylish home accessories. Some of these enterprises make their wares available in charming boutiques lining the main road from Seminyak up to Kerobokan

THIS PAGE (FROM TOP): A sidewalk stall in Kuta offers colourful kites; Haveli shows the sophisticated side of shopping in south Bali.

OPPOSITE (FROM TOP): Bali's southern beaches are a hit with surfers from around the world; dining al fresco as the sun sets can be a daily indulgence.

and beyond. Others are invisible, nestled in numerous workshops found along the back roads, focusing solely on their growing export markets.

The retail districts of Legian, Seminyak and Kerobokan in particular have become the market place of Indonesia. You will find a greater variety of antiques, crafts and furniture here than in any other single location in Indonesia. Professional buyers are well served by the incredible array of sometimes chaotic and dirty outlets lining the main streets and alleys of this area, which offer products from every corner of the extensive Indonesian archipelago.

Seminyak is also famous for being the town where 'Eat Street' can be found. The road's real name is Jalan Lesmana, or Jalan Oberoi. It runs from Seminyak's main road down to The Oberoi, and has seen restaurants popping up like mushrooms in recent years. On this single road you can now take your pick of Greek, Moroccan, Chinese, Italian, Indonesian, Japanese, American and Thai food, among others. Head down there on any given night and you're assured of some excellent international cuisine.

sanur: at a measured pace

The other coast of south Bali is a different world altogether. A single, winding road beneath leafy trees serves as the sole exit and entry point to the beach town of Sanur. It runs roughly parallel to the shore, and is lined on one side with boutique hotels, bungalows and the dignified residences of the lucky few who knew that Sanur was special decades ago. It is a quiet and slightly staid town, without a lot to see up front. What there is to see, is unobtrusive and never in-your-face like Kuta. Sanur is a little sleepy in comparison. The beaches are equally calm and reef-sheltered, with placid, shallow waters, and narrow stretches of beach.

Off the main street are shady lanes leading to the beaches, a few low-profile consulates, and the Batu Jimbar Estates, where some of the most illustrious characters from Bali's social and artistic scenes from decades past reside in quiet dignity. So if the kookiness of Kuta or the edginess of Seminyak are not your flavour, try Sanur instead.

denpasar: urban vortex

Bali's capital city of Denpasar is a chaotic vortex of Asian urbanism. The majority of its residents are non-Balinese due to intense immigration from other islands during recent years. Despite efforts by the local government to make it a destination for tourists, Denpasar remains primarily a place to get into and out of as quickly as possible.

But it still offers some interesting diversions. In the centre of the city are the Bali Arts Centre, the provincial arts college, and some of the island's oldest and most venerable palaces which are now private homes. There's also the Bali Museum, which houses some interesting artefacts. It sits beside one of the island's busiest temples. Shopping in downtown Denpasar offers some interesting opportunities, particularly in the big department stores, and electronics and outlet shops.

a cultural cocktail

Because its appeal is universal, south Bali has become a cultural crossroads, with not just one culture, but many, co-existing in surprising harmony. It is a polyglot playground of micro-cultures including the surf, expatriate, café, high and counter cultures. Also in the mix is real Balinese culture with its never-ending cycle of ritual.

Come stay and play in Seminyak or Kuta and you might brush elbows with Bollywood movie stars, Brazilian models, Japanese nobility, Silicon Valley billionaires, Italian fashion designers, Malay princes and others from the jet set. Pick up a copy of one of the free local event guides, or consult a concierge, then launch yourself into the social and cultural life of south Bali. You could find yourself at a gallery opening, a book launch, a villa party or a drag show, chatting with gurus, newscasters, healers, heads of state, priests, farmers, film-makers, environmentalists, aid workers, dive masters and many other masters of disguise. It is indeed a heady mix.

The juxtaposition of different cultures will amuse and surprise you. Your Balinese housemaid will place offerings on your laptop computer to keep it from acting up, reciting ancient mantras and sprinkling holy water as well. In the morning, at a

THIS PAGE (FROM TOP): Pony carts, or dokar, still ply their trade in downtown Denpasar; a figure of a courtier at the Bali Museum.

OPPOSITE (FROM TOP): Catching the rays in Seminyak; the entrance to the Bali Museum stands on the site of the old Denpasar royal palace.

beachside café, as you burst the egg yolk on your Eggs Benedict, you may witness a Balinese community in traditional dress, bearing offerings, incense and effigies of their gods to the water's edge for a melasti purification ritual. They sit on the sand in prayer, oblivious to the surfers in loud shorts thrashing down the face of the waves immediately in front of their sacred offerings, and beside them on the sand, an assortment of European sunbathers, scantily clad and observing the proceedings.

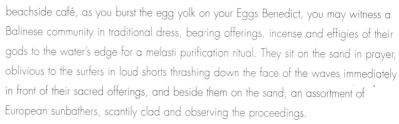

In south Bali, people simply smile and get on with their business, whatever that might be. The very best thing about the area's diversity is the peaceful way its contrasting elements blend together. There's an atmosphere of tolerance and mutual curiosity rather than one of judgement or tension. So stir it or shake it up, and pour it into a big, chilled glass. It is a delicious cultural cocktail.

cocktail culture

Back in the 1970s, south Bali was known for its shaggy-haired, beer-drinking culture, where surfers guzzled life straight from the bottle and slept in cheap bungalows under the coconut palms. That beer culture has been replaced by something more stylish, more edgy, and altogether more beau monde—cocktail culture. South Bali has become chic beyond belief. It has developed a new, luxe and lively lifestyle, with cocktail culture making its mark, particularly in this party zone.

It is a fun but ephemeral kind of culture which plays out against a backdrop of late-night bars, chill-out lounges, intimate soirées and villa entertaining—not to mention the fashion shows, cabaret shows and guest appearances by the hippest DJs from around the world, spinning new sounds every night. South Bali's cocktail culturists include fresh-eyed waifs and metrosexual bachelors who emerge nightly from their minimalist-cool villas to sip something chilled at one of the dozens of venues vying for their attention.

The epitome of this trend finds expression around sunset at Ku Dé Ta, a beachfront restaurant located next to The Oberoi in Seminyak. As the sky throws a rosy glow over the waves, seductive music throbs while a tantalisingly eclectic crowd of international

THIS PAGE: *Venues such as Hu'u Bar serve as stylish backdrops for hot conversations long into the night.*
OPPOSITE (FROM TOP): *A benevolent figure of Buddha at The Oberoi; the sunset scene at Ku Dé Ta.*

extraction reclines on the loungers, glasses in hand as laughter fills the air. The look is vaguely retro and ranges from funky T-shirts with clunky platforms, to Pucci minis, string bikinis with beads, and back again.

Variations of the Ku Dé Ta sunset theme are staged around the clock at other hot spots in the neighbourhood, from private villas to vast, ultra-modern clubs with illuminated bars serving flavoured oxygen on tap. There's always a party going on, and as long as you're on the island, you're also invited.

a day in the (night) life of south bali

The centre of south Bali's nightlife universe is a street called Jalan Dhyana Pura, which branches off the main road running from Legian to Seminyak. It was once a narrow, sandy lane sheltered by coconut palms, leading to the beach. It is still narrow, but the coconut trees are gone and both sides are packed with chic new clubs with names like Oxygen, Space, Spy Bar, Q Bar and Liquid.

Nightlife in Bali is relaxed and unintimidating. It is about easy mixing. And dressing up isn't as important as just turning up. The look is casual, fun, funky and sexy, or however you like. Wherever you go, you'll find an eclectic and friendly crowd, with locals, expatriates, Asians and Westerners in equal proportion. Some are younger, others older, some are straighter and others more gay. The only constant is the lateness of the hour, because these clubs don't start powering up until midnight, and often keep going until dawn. So come out and play, but it might help to pace yourself.

THIS PAGE (FROM TOP): DJs spin a soundtrack for the sunset on Seminyak beach; Ku Dé Ta's terraces are a hot zone during the day.
OPPOSITE (FROM TOP): Local brand Uluwatu combines traditional craftsmanship with modern style; Khaima's Moroccan flavours spice up the panoply of international cuisines offered along Eat Street.

party dregs meet the dawn patrol

When the bars sweep you out onto the street with the last of the party crowd, and the sun is making its ascent, you'll find the day's first surfers already on the water from Kuta to Canggu, catching a few smooth rides while the sea is still glassy. They're a mix of locals and foreigners, both

young and old. With several professional surf schools located on the beach in Kuta and Legian, just about anyone can learn. Some of the schools guarantee you'll catch a wave whether you're six or sixty years old.

Soon after the surfers, young kids and couples come out to swim or walk along the miles of wide and sandy shore before having breakfast at a beachside café or hotel in Seminyak. You sip a doppio cappucino while watching fishermen paddle out to set their nets, then you let your eyes follow along as a Brazilian beauty strides beside the waves with two perfectly groomed golden retrievers.

A group of Arabian horses canter past on a two-hour beach excursion out of a nearby stable, ridden by smart looking ladies from Perth, with a Balinese trainer close beside them. He's impeccably attired and handles his horse masterfully. The ladies are just getting the measure of their mounts while they take in the spaciousness of the south Bali strand, stretching out towards the volcanic peaks visible in the distance.

surviving a shopping safari on treasure island

As the hours fly by, the temperature rises. If you're going to shop, do yourself a favour and get started before it gets too hot. That way you can prowl the boutiques and warehouses of Seminyak and Kerobokan searching for antiques or that perfect Bali memento without fainting from heat exhaustion.

Shopping in south Bali gives new meaning to the phrase 'shop 'til you drop'. Authentic masterpieces of ancient and colonial cultures compete for attention with fabulous fakes and just plain junk from every corner of the Indonesian archipelago. Caveat emptor is the catchphrase for the astute shopper, but don't let that stop you from enjoying the search as you meander through side roads and alleys looking for hidden treasures. While Seminyak and Kerobokan are hot spots, there are plenty of antique vendors along the bypass road running from Nusa Dua to Sanur, and down the narrow roads of Kuta too. Exploration and endurance will surely be rewarded if your bargaining skills are bold and brash enough to close a sale at the right price.

When your hands are too filthy and your shirt is soaked through, instruct your driver to take you to a cool, modern café along the main road for lunch, or plop yourself down on a plain, wooden bench in a Balinese warung for an outrageously spicy nasi campur—a serving of rice accompanied by various local specialities and deliciously fiery sambal, the traditional local garnish.

mad dogs and englishmen

At the height of the day, take shelter in your hotel suite or breezy villa to snooze and catch the news via satellite. As you settle in, feeling cool and comfortable, across the island several sun-loving Brits are baking on the beach in Sanur, perfectly happy in the heat with a chilled beer each. It is peaceful as only Sanur can be. In the shade beneath their loungers, an assortment of Balinese dogs are stretched out. They may be a bit scruffy, but none of them are mad.

revival of the fittest

To prepare for another night out, you'll require some rejuvenation after your midday siesta. This is the moment for the Bali spa experience, and in south Bali you'll be spoiled for choice. Get a massage or enjoy a session of foot reflexology, and try some beauty treatments in preparation for making the scene again as the evening approaches. The spas of south Bali offer excellent value and the service is splendid.

When you're fully refreshed, meet friends at Seminyak's Eat Street for dinner, or sit back for a stunning sunset at Jimbaran Bay, where simple, locally-owned cafés serve you directly on the beach. The style is waxed canvas and plastic chairs, but the fish, grilled over coconut husk fires to smoky perfection, is supremely fresh. Your after-dinner options include a gallery opening, a fashion show, a poolside villa party, a full moon beach rave, a cabaret stage show, plus the excitement of all the clubs you didn't visit the night before. As the moon rises, you'll be refreshed, refuelled and ready for another night out in south Bali, the island's non-stop party zone.

THIS PAGE (FROM TOP): *Recover from an intense day and night in south Bali with a treatment at Henna Spa; culinary standards in south Bali are high and epitomised by classic presentation and meticulous preparation.*

OPPOSITE: *Take your languorous midday nap by The Oberoi's pool .*

...refreshed, refuelled and ready for another night out in south Bali...

The Avatara

THIS PAGE: *Panoramic views of Mount Batukau and the Sungi River await at The Avatara.*
OPPOSITE: *This impressive house lets you unwind in total privacy.*

Many savvy visitors to the Island of the Gods these days are eschewing the formality of resort properties and are instead embracing the more personal world of the private villa, of which there are a growing number in Bali. Often, it makes sense on many levels to choose to go in this direction—certainly it can offer better value for your money if you intend to travel with a group of friends or your family. And if it is privacy and informality you crave, then renting your own house in paradise is without a doubt the preferred option.

The choice of private villa makes all the difference, of course, and The Avatara ranks high on the list of Bali's sumptuous private leasing market. A magnificent house situated in a hidden area of Nyanyi, five minutes from the famous Tanah Lot temple, this charming mansion offers guests a chance to recharge the mind, body and spirit in luxurious seclusion overlooking the gently flowing Sungi River.

A vacation in a private villa like this adds an air of informality with its lack of restrictions. You'll sleep peacefully at night knowing there are no check-in or check-out times, no strangers to deal with and no limitations on when you can use the pool or when you eat (how many of us have missed the 11 am breakfast buffet deadline?). Then there's the best reason for choosing to go private—the property is ostensibly yours. You're free to do what you want, when you want.

From the moment you enter The Avatara—via a riverstone walkway that cuts

You're free to do what you want, when you want.

through scented water gardens—you'll know you've made a good choice. The villa was architecturally designed with ultimate guest comfort and privacy in mind. Surrounded by frangipani trees, it offers uninterrupted, picturesque views of the tropical surroundings—out towards dramatic Mount Batukau and over the Sungi. Realising that guests would enjoy this beautiful waterway, the owners built a flight of stone steps leading down to the banks of the river. Here, next to the bubbling water, you will find a comfortable Balinese

pavilion—the ultimate venue for intimate dinners or relaxing afternoon naps.

Designed by New Zealand architect Ross Franklin, The Avatara represents a fascinating mix of Balinese and Western styles. Back at the main house, interiors are flooded with an abundance of natural light, and feature white Balinese stone and carved volcanic rock. The stunning décor successfully embraces both traditional Balinese culture and modern luxury.

There are four separate guest suites at the villa, designed to accommodate up to

...The Avatara is surely a stand-out choice in the private villa stakes.

THIS PAGE (CLOCKWISE FROM RIGHT):
All four suites at The Avatara have teak floors and verandah doors that open onto the gardens and beyond; The Avatara, with its mix of Western and Balinese styles, offers tropical surroundings and modern comfort.

OPPOSITE: *A magnificent dining room seats 12.*

eight people. Two suites upstairs (Mountain View and Forest View) each have a king-size bed, while the two suites downstairs (Balé and River) feature one queen-size and two super-single beds. Each suite has its own individually designed bathroom. All are completely different yet equally stunning.

The guest suites also boast teak floors, floor-to-ceiling glass doors, and views of the villa's enticing infinity-edged swimming pool and gardens. An expansive dining area seats 12 comfortably and opens onto a private terrace overlooking the pool and riverbank forest beyond. Here, you can enjoy meals prepared by The Avatara's chef and his staff, cooked to suit your preferences. An extensive menu featuring Indonesian, Western, Chinese and vegetarian dishes is available. Should you choose to, you can take over the kitchen and prepare your own meals as well.

Linens are crisp and white, towels are fluffy and the helpful staff ensure there are always fresh flowers in your room. There's also every modern convenience you can think of available in your suite: a CD sound system, satellite television, air-conditioning, DVD player, ceiling fans, telephones, reading lamps and even those dreaded alarm clocks, should you need one.

Such amenities make The Avatara a popular choice with families. In fact, the kids will love a holiday in Bali simply because they will be revered as little gods. The locals believe that a child should not touch the ground during the first years of his or her life because the earth houses malevolent spirits. As a result, young children are carried everywhere until they reach the age of two, when a ceremony is held to protect the child from this first contact with 'evil'. These dark forces are not feared as they would be in the West, however, but embraced as equally important as the forces of good. It is a marriage best embodied in the yin-yang symbol; evidence of which you will find in many homes and private villas in Bali.

With everything you could need for a well-deserved break, The Avatara is surely a stand-out choice in the private villa stakes.

PHOTOGRAPHS COURTESY OF THE AVATARA.

FACTS

ROOMS	4 suites
FOOD	Indonesian • Western • Asian • vegetarian • special diets
DRINK	fully stocked fridge and extensive beverage menu
FEATURES	pool • biking • river walks • library • chauffeur-driven car
BUSINESS	Internet access
NEARBY	Tanah Lot • golf • horseback riding • cultural tours
CONTACT	Banjar Nyanyi, Desa Beraban, Tabanan 82121 • telephone: +62.361.754 344 • facsimile: +62.361.752 744 • email: info@theavatara.com • website: www.theavatara.com

Bali Niksoma

THIS PAGE: *Guests can laze around not one but two of such stunning swimming pools at Bali Niksoma.*

OPPOSITE: *The contemporary Balinese style evident throughout the hotel is the work of prominent Indonesian architect Hadi Prana.*

If the name Niksoma rings a bell, it is most likely because Bali Niksoma is a revamped version of a previous property—one of the oldest hotels in the Kuta and Legian area in fact—which now puts it in the category of a luxury hotel and wellness centre.

Credit for its improved appearance goes to the reputable Indonesian architect Hadi Prana, whose name ranks among the more luminary designers devoted to styling entire living spaces with a keen vision of how these might engage and elevate the

senses. Here, the vivid expression of a modern, tropical Balinese sensibility gives the resort a somewhat calming atmosphere. From the satisfying sense of serenity that prevails indoors, to the endless ocean view that greets guests at either of the two swimming pools, there's every reason to wish Bali Niksoma could be your real home.

There are 57 rooms available here, with an assortment of Standard and Deluxe Rooms, Junior Suites, suites and a spacious Presidential Villa. Every room comes with basic facilities such as an inviting four-poster king-size bed, satellite television, a wide balcony or terrace and a luxurious bathroom, of course. The Presidential Villa is a particularly memorable choice and suits families and groups of friends in particular, as it comes with two comfortable bedrooms and a private swimming pool.

Like much of traditional Bali, the resort's interior design emphasises the beauty and harmony of flowing spaces, but in a contemporary manner—an aesthetic and architectural principle that explains the rationale behind the clean, geometric lines and forms found indoors. This modern simplicity, however, is given a tropical twist with the choice of materials used: wood, stone and thatch have been combined to underscore the inspiration drawn from Bali's lush, green backdrop. Finally, the attraction

of the place is further augmented by the sensitive channelling of natural light and various modes of artificial ambient lighting.

The resort's convenient location along the beach at Legian is yet another pull factor. From this point, guests are privy to Bali's picturesque sunsets over the Indian Ocean. This will, without a doubt, inspire the trigger-happy among you. To maximise the stunning location, ocean views abound from every possible vantage point, including the rooms.

This is also a beach that is legendary with international surfers seeking to give their trusty old boards a seasonal spin.

Among the hotel's other outdoor features are two swimming pools, both overlooking the ocean, but one comes with an adjoining children's pool. Spacious walkways and terraces, and an expansive lawn, provide ample opportunities for leisurely strolls and fun games with the kids, who will surely enjoy running around freely.

The second advantage of its location is that the hotel is in close proximity to a number of gourmet restaurants, cafés and nightclubs. The main shopping belt is not far away either. Given the hotel's central location, it makes great sense, too, for tour operators to base their day tours here. This means a range of packaged tours are readily available to meet various interests, such as Balinese culture, nature or shopping.

Back at the resort, guests can savour the international fare at Hitana Restaurant and

THIS PAGE (TOP) AND OPPOSITE: Hitana Restaurant and Bar offers guests the perfect spot at which to enjoy their meals and a selection of cocktails when night falls.
BELOW: All rooms feature king-size beds and large bathrooms.

Bar. There is a diverse selection of Asian and Western à la carte offerings to be enjoyed here, in a spacious pavilion with high ceilings and a view of the ocean. A good selection of wine adds the finishing touch to a satisfying meal .

The Spa at Bali Niksoma is a haven for the world-weary. With three private spa suites equipped with showers and outdoor bathtubs, a gymnasium and a sauna, rest assured you'll enjoy a totally rejuvenating experience here. The spa menu includes a variety of massages, body wraps and scrubs, along with beauty treatments such as facials, manicures and pedicures. Do try one of their Royal Packages—The Niksoma Indulgence. This thorough and extensive 180-minute package includes a footbath, lavender body wash, traditional Balinese

...an excellent choice for those visiting Bali for the first time...

massage, a body scrub and conditioning treatment, floral bath and a face refresher (a conditioning treatment that uses a blend of fresh fruits and vegetables). You'll also be served ginger tea and cookies during a short break. If you can't get enough of the spa treatments, spend some time soaking in the hotel's outdoor jacuzzi.

With its proximity to the beach and some of Bali's liveliest areas, along with the facilities and services expected of a luxury hotel, including a family-friendly set-up, Bali Niksoma is an execellent choice for those visiting Bali for the first time, or those who enjoy their holidays in the thick of things.

FACTS

ROOMS	10 Standard Rooms • 34 Deluxe Rooms • 8 Junior Suites • 4 Suites • 1 Presidential Villa
FOOD	Hitana Restaurant and Bar: Asian and international
DRINK	restaurant bar • mini-bar
FEATURES	pool • spa • beach • gymnasium • sauna • jacuzzi
BUSINESS	Internet access
NEARBY	restaurants • cafés • shopping
CONTACT	Jalan Padma Utara, Legian Kaja, Legian 80361 • telephone: +62.361.751 946 • facsimile: +62. 361.753 587 • email: baliniksoma@indosat.net.id • website: www.baliniksoma.com

PHOTOGRAPHS COURTESY OF BALI NIKSOMA.

The Club at The Legian

While this hotel operates as a kind of private clubhouse, it is still a great spot for families and corporate retreat groups who remain deeply appreciative of the kind of fussing and fawning, and the many little luxuries usually offered by larger hotels.

Situated just across the street from its sister property, The Legian, The Club at The Legian is a new addition that raises the level of exclusivity up a few notches. While The Legian is located along Seminyak Beach in Bali's south, The Club is just across the street and a short walk away from the same sparkling sands of Seminyak. Guests at The Club are welcome to use The Legian's beach and pool, and a buggy service between the two properties ensures you have no reason not to take in the beautiful surroundings.

There are 10 one-bedroom villas at The Club and one larger three-bedroom villa, all

of them housed within private compounds that include a 10-m (33-ft) swimming pool, two day beds and an outdoor dining bale overlooking the pool. Among the in-room features you can expect are a Bose home theatre system, cable television and your own espresso machine. Also provided are the usual comforts such as daily newspapers, American breakfasts, laundry service and a well-stocked mini-bar. For added convenience, each villa has an appointed personal butler. Guests will also find sensory satisfaction in the calm bodies of water that run around the bathroom and outdoor bathtub, accentuated with delightful pond ornaments, water plants and vibrant, tropical flowers.

A focal point of The Club, however, is the main swimming pool located just off to the right of the entrance. This visual treat more than makes up for the lack of a

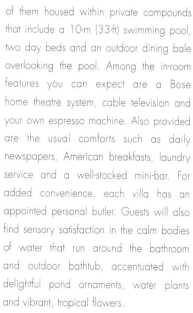

...raises the level of exclusivity up a few notches.

THIS PAGE (FROM TOP): *Enjoy a meal at The Club Lounge, overlooking the main pool; Asian aesthetics define the interiors, with Balinese materials used to create The Club's look and feel.*

OPPOSITE (FROM TOP): *Architect Shinta Siregar's love for bathroom design shines through here, with a focus on light, space and quality fixtures; day beds by the private pool allow for indulgent afternoon naps.*

beachfront at your doorstep. Overlooking the pool is The Club Lounge, where you can have your meals should you choose not to dine in the privacy of your villa.

If you need yet another reason to pick The Club, then the resort's limousine service is it. Running between Seminyak, Legian and Kuta, this service allows you to enjoy the best of Bali in luxurious comfort. From the tranquillity of Seminyak, and down to Legian and Kuta, you'll be able to take in the sights and sounds from your limousine, hopping out as and when you please to get a snack or shop around. This is just one of those extra touches that make The Club at The Legian the right choice.

FACTS		
ROOMS	10 one-bedroom villas • 1 three-bedroom villa
FOOD	The Club Lounge: Western and Asian
DRINK	The Club Lounge • mini-bar
FEATURES	private pool • outdoor bathtub • personal butler • home theatre system • limousine service
BUSINESS	2 meetings room at The Legian
NEARBY	Seminyak Beach • Legian • Kuta
CONTACT	Jalan Laksmana, Seminyak Beach 80361 • telephone: +62.361.730 622 • facsimile: +62.361.730 623 • email: legian@ghmhotels.com • website: www.ghmhotels.com

PHOTOGRAPHS COURTESY OF THE CLUB AT THE LEGIAN.

Hotel Tugu Bali

THIS PAGE: *Dinner and drinks on the beach are an enticing prospect at Hotel Tugu Bali.*

OPPOSITE: *Puri Le Mayeur is a honeymooner's villa built over a natural lotus pond, where guests enjoy the added luxury of a private dining pavilion.*

Hotel Tugu Bali is located on a secluded stretch of beach in the quaint fishing village of Canggu—a small settlement with a romantic, timeless quality along Bali's south coast. Its 22 private villas and suites, housed in traditional Balinese huts surrounded by wild lotus ponds have been designed to emphasise their unique character.

For all the peace and quiet guests can enjoy here, the primary attraction of this hotel, however, is something undefinable that guests begin to feel as soon as they enter the lobby. Whether it is the atmosphere of tropical exoticism, timelessness, spirituality or perhaps a well-balanced combination of all of the above, few guests care to find the answer as they unconsciously say goodbye to the hustle and bustle of the modern world, and step into the world of Tugu.

Hotel Tugu Bali is the product of a long, loving relationship between a lawyer and antique collector, Anhar Setjadibrata, and the rich, artistic history of Indonesia. As a struggling student in Java in the 1960s, he always found the time and commitment to develop his passion for the indigenous art and history of his country. This interest led him to invest in his first batch of antiques, a move that launched an extremely personal collection that continues to grow in size and significance. His desire to share his stunning collection with the world resulted in the establishment of Hotel Tugu Bali in 1997.

Not satisfied with the beautiful displays of genuine antiques here, Anhar moved an authentic 300-year-old Peranakan ancestral temple to the hotel, calling it Bale Sutra, or the Palace of Harmony. An intriguing display of vintage photographs, original Peranakan gold-embroidered-silk textiles, and statues of

...housed in traditional Balinese huts surrounded by wild lotus ponds...

Chinese-influenced deities give this hall a regal character. The red-walled temple now hosts tantalising dinners and spectacular wedding ceremonies, where Balinese suckling pigs are carved under a centuries-old statue of the Goddess of Mercy.

Indonesian art and culture pervade in the villas as well, with a prime example being the romantic Puri Le Mayeur, an ocean-view villa that pays homage to the love story of Adrien Jean Le Mayeur de Merprés, a Belgian painter who made Bali his home, and Ni Polok, the beautiful Balinese dancer who became his wife. The villa houses items Ni Polok left to Anhar.

The Walter Spies Pavilion is another unique villa. It recreates the German artist's home in Yogyakarta, Central Java, in the 1930s. Decorated with Art Deco furniture, chandeliers, stained-glass windows, and the artist's memorabilia—an old camera, personal correspondence, photographs and

an experience coloured by your chosen dining venue. First on the list is Waroeng Tugu, a local-style eatery with a traditional village kitchen that no longer exists in modern Indonesia. With long wooden benches, terracotta pots, charcoal stoves, oil lamps and bamboo steamers, this 'waroeng' recreates a dining experience that was typical during the Majapahit era.

Whether you're savouring an authentic Indonesian meal in Waroeng Tugu, a formal Balinese megibung in Bale Agung, a traditional Peranakan feast in Bale Sutra, or a barbecue with freshly caught seafood on the beach, you will leave with a distinct impression of both the food and the venue. Intimate candlelit dinners for two can be arranged anywhere on the property as well.

The spa at Hotel Tugu Bali is also filled with artistic treasures both indoors and outdoors, and offers authentic therapies and

paintings—this villa is styled like a Javanese pavilion and is surrounded by a garden.

The hotel also has a number of suites in which guests will find subtle luxuries. All suites on the first level feature limestone outdoor baths and private plunge pools, while the upper-level suites offer ocean views and a private spa area, with large, silver sunken tubs carved by local artisans.

Themed restaurants are another feature at Hotel Tugu, where each meal becomes

THIS PAGE: The vibrant look of the Dedari Suites features both outdoors and indoors, where natural light is enhanced by the use of yellows and greens.

OPPOSITE: An ornate doorway marks the entrance to an opulent bedroom.

treatments inherited from ancient Javanese and Balinese royalty. The extensive menu at Waroeng Djamoe Spa also includes Eastern aromatherapies which focus on both the spiritual and the physical, using various roots and flowers that are believed to have healing powers. Rose petals are scattered every night in the bedrooms not only to invite romance but also for their scent which is believed to awaken the heart's chakra, making one more open to love.

Signature treatments here include the Balinese dancing massage where therapists fuse dance rituals with relaxation therapies, accompanied by Balinese music. Also a highlight is the hot stone massage which uses volcanic stones from Java and the Yangtze River in China.

Judging by the change guests undergo while staying at Hotel Tugu Bali, Anhar is well on his way to ensuring continued recognition for Indonesian artists, and the foreign talents the region has nurtured.

PHOTOGRAPHS COURTESY OF HOTEL TUGU BALI.

FACTS	
ROOMS	10 Rejang Suites • 9 Dedari Suites • 1 Family Suite • 1 Walter Spies Pavilion • 1 Puri Le Mayeur
FOOD	Waroeng Tugu: Javanese • Bale Sutra: Peranakan • Bale Puputan: Indonesian • Bale Agung: megibung
DRINK	bar • wine cellar
FEATURES	pool • spa • beach • library • art shop • biking
BUSINESS	business centre • Internet access
NEARBY	Batu Bolong • Canggu village
CONTACT	Jalan Pantai Batu Bolong, Canggu 80361 • telephone: +62.361.731 701 • facsimile: +62.361.731 704 • email: bali@tuguhotels.com • website: www.tuguhotels.com

The Istana

Located within the spiritual sphere of Pura Uluwatu at Bali's southern tip, The Istana is a private villa offering five-star perks.

Its five suites—one master suite and four bedroom suites, two facing the ocean and two with garden views—are housed on a 5,200 sq m (6,219 sq yd) clifftop property which offers a priceless, panoramic view of the peninsula. White-sand beaches, a lagoon filled with corals and marine life, and spectacular sunsets are just some of the attractions you can enjoy at The Istana.

It is not just the guarantee of golden sunsets that distinguishes this property from the rest, however. Spacious interiors are furnished with earthy materials like teak and limestone, while rich fabrics with intricate patterns and weaves add a touch of colour.

The villa bears an equal balance of European influences and Asian aesthetics— the former is manifested in the unwavering attention to luxury and detail, while the latter is visible in the sensitive application of earth tones and natural textures which pay

THIS PAGE: *The stand-alone master suite has its own entrance and offers a little more privacy.*
OPPOSITE *The villa's split-level grounds offer stunning views of the Indian Ocean.*

...The Istana is a private villa offering five-star perks.

creative tribute to the lush landscape that dominates the area. This homage to Bali's natural charms is enhanced by strategically placed Indonesian primitive art which showcases the attractive mysticism that defines the Island of the Gods.

The main house consists of a living and dining room, an entertainment area and four bedroom suites. A highlight here is the white limestone carving on the living room's right wall. This arresting centrepiece depicts the first arrival of the pioneering priest Pedanda Sakti Wawu Rauh who travelled to Bali from Java in the 16th century and attained his spiritual fulfilment at the very same spot where the sacred Pura Uluwatu temple, revered by the locals, was later erected.

The dining room, seating 10, overlooks lily-filled ponds on one side and the ocean on the other. A bar is conveniently located here as well and comes stocked with international wines, spirits and mixers. The entertainment area, or Dotcom room, is where you'll find a massive couch covered with Thai silk pillows facing a wide-screen television and home theatre system. Behind the couch you'll find a cosy study area with a computer that is conveniently equipped with high-speed Internet access.

The master suite is in a separate guest house accessed by a walkway near the main entrance. Among its features are a sheltered deck, swimming pool, outdoor shower, day bed and kitchenette. The four bedroom suites are just as luxurious, with sunken bathtubs and private courtyards.

Outside, guests will find the extensive grounds spread over two levels. The upper-level garden has a bed of thick, soft grass, with coconut trees and lotus-filled ponds adding a tropical feel. The lower level has a sprawling lawn suitable for weddings, cocktail parties or a simple game of tag with your children. The villa's main swimming pool overlooks the ocean and separates the garden from the lawn.

As can be expected of a private villa like this, guests are assured of all creature comforts, including tantalising meals. The villa's hospitality team ensures exceptional cuisine and full butler service, which comes in handy if you are travelling with children. Various set menus are available, along with an à la carte selection and an enticing menu for the young ones. Special diets can be accommodated with no fuss as well. All you have to do is make your choice and sit back as the chef whips up a feast. The kitchen is also at your disposal should you decide to cook something yourself.

With the range of services and facilities provided, The Istana has made it possible for guests to never leave the villa's grounds. Spa treatments ranging from massages, to body scrubs and wraps, facials, manicures, and pedicures, and even hair braiding can be arranged at your convenience, in-house. And if you think the children might get bored, there's no need to worry because in addition to the pool, which always keeps them occupied, the Dotcom room comes equipped with a Sony Playstation and a library of DVDs, CDs and books.

Should you, however, feel the need to leave your private paradise during the day, a chauffeur is available to drive you to an intimate dinner at any of the restaurants nearby, or to take in Bali's historical and cultural sights. The luxury vehicle used is family-friendly and seats seven comfortably. Additional vehicles and drivers can be arranged as well. If you'd like to leave the children behind for the day, The Istana's

capable staff will gladly keep an eye on them, making sure they are sufficiently entertained and that they stay out of harm's way. Family-friendly service indeed!

With such attention paid to every little detail and its ability to anticipate your every need, The Istana is a great choice whether you are travelling with family or friends, and is also one of the many reasons why a lot of visitors are choosing to go the private villa route when heading to Bali.

THIS PAGE: Sliding glass doors in the bedrooms open onto the garden.

OPPOSITE (FROM TOP): The Istana's chefs create dishes worthy of any fine dining restaurant; the master suite, with its extra facilities, is a haven for parents looking for a little quality time away from the children.

PHOTOGRAPHS COURTESY OF THE ISTANA.

FACTS

ROOMS	1 master suite • 4 bedroom suites
FOOD	Indonesian • Western • Asian • vegetarian • special diets
DRINK	fully-stocked bar
FEATURES	pool • Dotcom room • chauffeur-driven car
BUSINESS	Internet access
NEARBY	Pura Uluwatu • beach • surfing
CONTACT	Jalan Labuan Sait, Pantai Suluban, Uluwatu 80361 • telephone: +62.361.730 668 • facsimile: +62.361.736 566 • email: agents@balihomes.com • website: www.theistana.com

The Legian

THIS PAGE: *The Legian's mix of the traditional and modern is attributed to Indonesian designer Hadi Prana.*

OPPOSITE (FROM TOP): *The Restaurant overlooks the pool and serves a varied menu; The Legian's suites reflect the 'indigenous modern' spirit; guests can indulge in spa therapies and cuisine at The Spa at The Legian.*

Situated close to Bali's colourful shopping and entertainment belt in the south, yet far enough away from the madding crowds to offer the seclusion of a completely different world, The Legian, in Seminyak, is one of those popular resorts that surface regularly when people begin inevitable discussions about where one should stay in Bali.

It is a quest that can often lead to protracted opinions, given the number of people who have spent time on the Island of the Gods, and the variety of excellent properties there. As a result, these chats can often go on endlessly. Yet it would be doing a potential visitor a great disservice not to put this superb resort on any list of accommodation possibilities.

The Legian is a unique property; the kind of place that feels more like a private residence than a formal hotel. Operated by

...the kind of place that feels more like a private residence than a formal hotel.

General Hotels Management, a well-known boutique resort company with a reputation for combining modern design and excellent service, the hotel is set in tranquil gardens right on the beach and offers an imposing grandeur while delivering an experience that is extremely personal and inviting.

There are many little touches at The Legian which instantly set it apart from the mainstream. It is clear as soon as you arrive that considerable effort has been made to create something different. The architecture, for one, immediately strikes the right note, giving guests a taste of what lies within. Designed by Indonesian Hadi Prana, the resort is a bold but essential marriage of the traditional and modern—it feels exclusive, yet exudes a sense of refinement that brings to mind a private palace.

The grand entrance is an elegant combination of muted colours and ordered simplicity, with interior furnishings and timber pieces created by Jaya Ibrahim, another well-known name in the Indonesian design circle. Ibrahim, who spent 10 years in the UK working with designer Anouska Hempel, makes a contemporary reinterpretation of Indonesia's traditional designs and marries them with modern materials to produce a new sense of tropical chic.

This spirit of 'indigenous modern' extends to the exclusive accommodation.

Each of The Legian's 67 suites—there are only suites, and they are huge—is furnished with a rich combination of old and new. Polished woods and cool marble are complemented by Indonesian fabrics and artefacts, giving this seaside residence a luxurious and unique feel.

Choose between one of 15 airy Studio Suites with separate bathrooms, twin vanities, a charming living area and a spacious balcony overlooking the Indian Ocean; or stay in one of the hotel's larger one- or two-bedroom suites, suitable for families or groups of friends.

Two luxury apartments, The Legian and The Seminyak Suites, offer more space than most of us enjoy at home, and a level of

...dine in the privacy of your suite or al fresco on your breezy balcony...

luxury few will ever experience. Each of these exquisite suites has two comfortable bedrooms, double balconies and an ocean-view terrace for sunbathing or dining. The Legian Suite has more than 360 sq m (3,875 sq ft) of living space overlooking the hotel's pool and the Indian Ocean, which laps calmly at the foot of the property along a spectacular, golden-sand beach. It is the same view available to all of the suites at The Legian. Balcony-living here is an experience not to be missed.

On the ground floor, The Spa at The Legian has an inviting range of uniquely relaxing massages, exotic Indonesian treatments and much more. Some of the very enticing spa treatments available include Ayurvedic Rejuvenation Therapy, Warm Stone Massage and foot reflexology. A wholesome and healthy spa cuisine menu completes the indulging experience.

Spa cuisine is not the only food you'll find at The Legian. The Restaurant, which opens onto the pool terrace, serves a menu of healthy breakfasts, light lunches or romantic dinners, with a selection that includes a choice of exquisite modern cuisine, traditional Indonesian specialities and other Asian dishes. An open kitchen lets you inside the workings of this brasserie-style restaurant and lends a casual atmosphere to dining out. Of course, you may also wish

to dine in the privacy of your suite or al fresco on your breezy balcony for a truly romantic setting.

While The Legian offers seclusion in abundance, it is also within easy reach of the vibrant shopping and nightlife districts of Seminyak, Legian and Kuta. Bali's artistic centre of Ubud—which was once the home of famous painters Walter Spies and Rudolph Bonnet—is less than an hour's drive

away, and a detour through the back roads gives visitors a view of rural Bali. Within a day's drive, the spectacular volcanic central highlands have their own appeal.

Tucked away along the secluded southern tip of the island and flanked by a quiet beach and lush rice terraces, The Legian offers a unique chance to experience Bali's magical charms in a relaxed and personal setting.

THIS PAGE: Guests can spend the day lazing under the sun with a stunning view of the beach in front of them.

OPPOSITE (FROM TOP): As with the rest of the property, the suites feature a mix of the traditional and contemporary; dining on the beach is a pleasure few guests can resist.

PHOTOGRAPHS COURTESY OF THE LEGIAN.

FACTS		
ROOMS	67 suites	
FOOD	The Restaurant: modern cuisine	
DRINK	The Lobby Lounge and Bar: cocktails and cigars • The Pool Bar: cocktails, lunch menu and snacks	
FEATURES	pool • spa • gym • boutique • hospitality suite • yoga	
BUSINESS	conference facilities • 2 meeting rooms	
NEARBY	shopping • nightlife • beach • restaurants	
CONTACT	Jalan Laksmana, Seminyak Beach 80361 • telephone: +62.361.730 622 • facsimile: +62.361.730 623 • email: legian@ghmhotels.com • website: www.ghmhotels.com	

The Oberoi, Bali

THIS PAGE: *Guests can expect exclusive luxury at The Oberoi, where private villas are set within mature gardens believed to have a beneficial effect on spiritual well-being.*

OPPOSITE: *A high regard for local culture has gained The Oberoi a reputation as one of Bali's most enduring and scenic private compounds.*

The island's spiritual side comes to the fore at The Oberoi, Bali; without a doubt one of Indonesia's most exclusive and beautiful resort properties.

The beach fronting the hotel is considered among the holiest on Bali's western coast. It is revered by the Balinese as a sacred place and marked by an important temple, Pura Petitenget. Legend has it that a 15th-century Balinese priest, Ida Pedanda Sakti Waurauh, took a break close to The Oberoi's beach while on a pilgrimage from Tanah Lot in the northwest of the island, to Uluwatu in the south. Over 600 years later, worshippers and tourists alike still flock to the traditional temple erected in his honour, and almost daily, a colourful procession sweeps past the stunning property to the secluded 500-m (547-yd) beach.

Built almost 30 years ago as a private club and later converted into a luxury resort, The Oberoi's charm lies primarily in its tranquil and impeccable setting along northern Seminyak Beach, one of the most beautiful beaches on the island. Days spent here are nothing short of idyllic, and it's hardly surprising to discover that the hotel counts among its clientele many of the world's best-known celebrities.

The Oberoi's six hectares (15 acres) of mature, tropical gardens are believed to provide the necessary conditions for spiritual well-being. The serene setting provided by these gardens is perfectly complemented by the resort's luxurious look and feel. Here, local architecture meets modern style in a magnificent match. Fifteen superb thatched villas are enclosed within private, coral-walled courtyards reminiscent of traditional Balinese compounds, each housing a dining pavilion, an air-conditioned bedroom and en suite bathroom. Nine of these villas have a private, full-size swimming pool just a few steps away from the bedroom.

The Oberoi's 60 Lanai rooms are as comfortable as the villas, each featuring a terrace for outdoor dining and a luxurious, air-conditioned bathroom with a sunken bath. Elegant furnishings such as teak beds and cool, marble floors add to the opulent surroundings.

...one of the most enduring private compounds on the Island of the Gods.

The resort's natural beauty provides the perfect setting for a meal at the beachside Frangipani Café. Here you can enjoy breakfast under the trees while taking in the sights and sounds of Seminyak Beach. After a lazy afternoon spent idling by the pool, a perfect evening might encompass knotting a sarong around your waist and strolling over to the laid-back Kayu Bar for a cocktail.

From there, you might walk barefoot back to your exclusive villa for a refreshing shower and a change of clothes. A dinner featuring a spread of international cuisine awaits at The Oberoi's acclaimed signature restaurant, The Kura Kura.

After a satisfying meal, stroll through the gardens to the hotel's private amphitheatre to enjoy performances staged beneath the night sky. To the crash of a gamelan orchestra, dancers will weave and swirl in an entrancing and magical show.

The allure of island life is enhanced at The Oberoi Spa by Banyan Tree. Guests can expect a unique combination of

THIS PAGE: *Inside, guests will appreciate the rich textures of Bali reflected in the furnishings, while outside, the resort's beautiful gardens create a sense of wonderful calm.*

OPPOSITE: *Enjoy breakfast at Frangipani Café and prepare for a relaxing day ahead.*

relaxation, rejuvenation and pampering techniques that result in first-class spa treatments. These can be enjoyed outdoors in two private massage pavilions within the spa's compound. Also available are a sauna, gymnasium and tennis court.

The Oberoi's attention to detail and respect for local culture has helped it establish a reputation as one of the most enduring private compounds on the Island of the Gods. Today, The Oberoi is consistently recognised by the travel industry for its exclusive brand of style and charm; a characteristic familiar to its many guests who return time and again to enjoy the resort's magnificent serenity. Among many other accolades, The Oberoi was recently picked by *Condé Nast Traveler* for inclusion in its prestigious Gold List, placing this resort alongside the world's very best.

In short, this upmarket establishment offers Bali's many visitors the chance to experience the island in its purest form.

PHOTOGRAPHS COURTESY OF THE OBEROI, BALI.

FACTS		
ROOMS	60 rooms • 15 villas
FOOD	Frangipani Café: fresh seafood and light meals • The Kura Kura: Indonesian, Asian and Continental
DRINK	Kayu Bar
FEATURES	pool • gardens • spa • beach • tennis
BUSINESS	Internet access
NEARBY	shops • bars • cafés • restaurants
CONTACT	Jalan Laksmana, Seminyak Beach 80361 • telephone: +62.361.730 361 • facsimile: +62.361.730 791 • email: reservations@theoberoi-bali.com • website: www.oberoihotels.com

Sienna Villas

As far as interiors go, Seminyak's Sienna Villas probably has the most distinctive and immediately recognisable look because of the exotice blend of influences—Balinese, Egyptian and Tunisian—found in its décor.

It is such details and the quality of your experience here that marks Sienna Villas as a true luxury villa. From stylish interiors in soothing tones of wood or natural finishes in stone, to the sun-kissed swimming pool and the comforts found in your luxurious villa, one experience flows into another with seamless ease. Simply stepping into the villa offers a visual treat as the view extends across the living area and out towards the pool. This juxtaposition of outdoor pleasures against indoor indulgences characterises a stay at Sienna Villas.

This luxury property comprises the four-bedroom Villa Puri Sienna, and Sienna Villas, which are four three-bedroom villas. Puri Sienna is designed to maximise privacy.

THIS PAGE (CLOCKWISE FROM RIGHT):
Enjoy a tantalising meal cooked by your villa's personal chef in a little gazebo; bedrooms feature a tasteful blend of design influences; the private pool sparkles with an emerald hue.
OPPOSITE: Tropical gardens provide a perfect backdrop for a day spent lazing by the main pool at Puri Sienna.

Three of its bedrooms are spread out generously within the villa's grounds, with the last bedroom located above the main house. Each bedroom, however, has easy access to the common facilities and also comes with a verandah suitable for intimate dinners. Should you want to dine with your family or friends instead, the gazebo is fitted with a dining table for eight, a sound system to set the mood with music, and barbecue facilities, all within the tropical confines of the villa's gardens. Puri Sienna comes with two pools—one in the main garden and the other in front of two of the master bedrooms.

The Sienna Villas, on the other hand, are sturdy, double-storey buildings with three bedrooms on the second level, all with king-size beds. Downstairs, a spacious living area leads to an outdoor deck surrounding an emerald-hued swimming pool which gets its mesmerising colour from jade and green stone sourced from Java. Inside each villa, guests can expect a fully-equipped kitchen, a dining room that seats six and an entertainment system which lets you to make the most of the expansive living area.

Both the Puri Sienna and Sienna Villas are serviced by staff who prepare breakfast daily, and can organise barbecues and private dinner parties at your request. On the barbecue menu are tasty options like marinated tuna in a special sauce, grilled prawns with a butter garlic sauce, and standard fare such as beef and chicken sausages, fried rice and salad. Those who love seafood will appreciate the grilled

THIS PAGE: *The uncluttered interior of the master bedroom is complemented by the use of warm, soothing colours and wood furnishings.*
OPPOSITE: *Loungers by the poolside prove too inviting to resist.*

marinated calamari in garlic and sweet soy sauce, and the grilled crab in a special butter sauce. If a taste of authentic Balinese cuisine is what you're after, tuck into dishes such as Be Sampi Mebasa Manis, which is beef cooked to tender perfection in spices and coconut milk, or Ayam Pelalah, chicken served in a sweet tomato sauce. These should be enjoyed with a steaming plate of nasi kuning, or yellow rice. As for dessert, try the Bubur Injin, a traditional black rice pudding served with coconut milk.

With notice, the team of personal chefs can prepare all your favourite dishes too. Guests can also tour the nearby markets to sample the local produce and perhaps even cook their own meals in the villa. Such explorations actually allow guests to better appreciate the local tastes and cultures in a way that no tour package can. Besides that, your new-found knowledge comes in a most tangible and tasty form. Alternatively, there are menus available from a number of leading restaurants within easy delivery distance. All you have to do is select your dishes and let the staff handle the rest.

Given that different villas inevitably appeal to different people, Sienna Villas is a choice venue for a group getaway. The villa's Australian manager has been known to demonstrate his skill and resourcefulness when organising shopping and cultural tours around the local area or beyond.

The property also regularly plays host to family reunions, birthday parties and corporate retreats, catering to guests from all over the world and all walks of life. Floating in the swimming pools, relaxing in the Balinese gazebo, indulging their appetites by the barbecue pits, or just strolling around the vicinity to the nearby beach, guests will quickly find the repose they deserve.

Sienna Villas is a popular spot with couples celebrating their weddings as well.

A complete package including the legal paperwork, wedding set-up, food and beverages, entertainment, photographer, hairdresser, flowers and transport can be organised by the capable staff here. Puri Sienna can be set up for both the ceremony and the reception because of its private compound and spacious grounds. Couples spending their honeymoon here will enjoy massages and a poolside dinner too.

For an intimate holiday in a centrally located villa offering first-class facilities, luxurious comfort and professional and friendly staff, you can't go wrong by choosing Sienna Villas.

FACTS		
	ROOMS	1 Puri Sienna Villa • 4 Sienna Villas
	FOOD	Balinese • international • barbecue
	DRINK	fully-stocked fridge
	FEATURES	private pool • personal chef • tours • massages • chauffeur-driven car
	NEARBY	beach • restaurants • temples • river rafting • golf • tennis • scuba diving
	CONTACT	No.5 Gang Keraton, Jalan Raya Seminyak, Seminyak 80361 • telephone: +62.361.734 698 • facsimile: +62.361.732 585 • email: info@sienna-villas.com • website: www.sienna-villas.com

PHOTOGRAPHS COURTESY OF SIENNA VILLAS.

Villa Balquisse

THIS PAGE (CLOCKWISE FROM TOP): *The open-air pavilions are perfect for a private yoga session; whether swimming in the private pool or relaxing on a lounger, guests will relish the feeling of tranquillity; quaint pathways allow for leisurely strolls throughout the day.*

OPPOSITE: *Distinctive Balinese architecture accounts for the breezy and spacious interiors.*

Regulars of Bali's hotel scene know Villa Balquisse as a palatial retreat located in the old fishing village of Jimbaran, amidst a rich landscape of mangrove and coconut trees. The hotel was conceptualised and built by Zohra Boukhari, its Moroccan-born owner, who continues to manage this estate with her husband Blaise as a labour of love. In fact, the hotel takes its name from the owner's daughter, Balquisse, who also shares it with a legendary queen in Muslim history. The couple's dedicated attention has earned the hotel enthusiastic accolades from travel and resort organisations across the world, and it is thus no surprise that travellers constantly arrive at Villa Balquisse's doorstep already familiar with its reputation for splendour and hospitality.

The most distinctive visual feature of Villa Balquisse remains its seamless marriage of local architecture with various Moroccan elements which have been brought together with nothing less than impeccable taste and a genuine boutique sensibility. In this vein, the main entrance to the hotel takes the form of a grand temple-like stone doorway, and stands as a portal to a world of rest and relaxation. Zohra's personal vision of luxurious villa living is expressed through the extensive collection of Oriental-style furniture which includes a large collection of antiques and antique reproductions.

Villa Balquisse is a cosy estate with an assortment of nine rooms in two villas. One villa houses four rooms, while the second villa comes with five rooms, all of which have one king-size bed. These rooms can be easily combined to offer guests a three-, four-, five-, seven- or nine-bedroom villa, should they be travelling in a large group. Each villa also has a private swimming pool lined with emerald-green natural stones and wooden decks filled with teak furniture.

Every room has a distinct visual style, with a unique colour scheme that ranges from burgundy to orange, yellow, blue, cream, dark orange, light orange and brownish-pink. These come together in a complementary colour palette to endow the estate with an earthy and tranquil mood.

The villas feature traditional architecture and an elegant interior décor with creative interpretations and applications of local visual styles, colours and materials such as coconut, tadalak, terracotta and stone. These have been transformed into unique living spaces with an exotic, yet homely atmosphere. Fabrics were sourced from far and wide to enhance the décor, and these range from Javanese silk to saris from Jaipur.

You'll find them used to create vibrant bedcovers and luxurious pillowcases.

The hotel's Garam Asam restaurant is well-known for its ingenious fusion cuisine and serves authentic Indonesian specialities as well as dishes with Indian, Southeast Asian, Middle Eastern and European influences. The delightful and varied menu indeed testifies to the creativity and expertise of the culinary crew. The in-house chef is a veteran who holds his own among the masters of the five-star hotel circuit, and he has designed a range of themed dining options such as a simple but moving Romantic Dinner, barbecue parties with meat and seafood marinated with herbs and spices, or a hearty Cuisine Under The Stars.

The in-house Henna Spa is another popular facility, offering a number of rejuvenating packages including the Balinese Boreh Royal Ritual, based on methods and recipes handed down from generation to generation of dedicated Balinese health practitioners. The hotel caters to business needs too with a well-equipped business centre.

THIS PAGE (FROM TOP):
Antique table-top accessories complete the exotic getaway experience; luxurious bedrooms showcase the different textures and patterns of fabrics sourced from around and beyond the region.
OPPOSITE: Living areas are visually intriguing thanks to the tasteful match of local and imported furnishings.

Whether you crave a stroll along the sandy beach, a mesmerising performance of magic tricks and illusions, or a Balinese wedding ceremony complete with the traditional solemnisation rites, the front desk will be able to oblige with due promptness.

Villa Balquisse is approximately 10 km (6 miles) from the airport, and provides easy access to the sights and sounds of southern Bali. The estate itself is surrounded by a natural landscape of tropical flora, and the nearby beach has been hailed as one of the more impressive stretches in Bali on account of its dazzling white sand and beautiful views of the clear, blue Indian Ocean. There is also a popular golf course at Nusa Dua to look forward to, and a wide range of exciting activities on the water to enjoy. These range from day cruises to diving expeditions and surfing. With such memorable experiences and attractions in store, Villa Balquisse indeed delivers a vacation like few others can.

FACTS		
	ROOMS	2 villas
	FOOD	fusion
	DRINK	restaurant bar
	FEATURES	pool • spa
	BUSINESS	business centre
	NEARBY	fishing village • Pura Uluwatu • Dreamland surfer's beach
	CONTACT	Jalan Uluwatu 18X, Jimbaran 80361 • telephone: +62.361.701 695 • facsimile: +62.361.701 695 • email: info@balquisse.com • website: www.balquisse.com

PHOTOGRAPHS COURTESY OF VILLA BALQUISSE.

The Villas Bali Hotel + Spa

If your spa sessions of late have left you feeling physically relaxed and rejuvenated but spiritually uninspired, a stay at The Villas Bali Hotel and Spa is just what you need. The distinctive décor at the spa creates a holistic and invigorating environment that works on your mind and spirit, while a team of professional therapists work to heal your body. In fact, a stint at The Villas Bali will effectively arouse your senses and leave you with a greater awareness of, and new appreciation for the innovation of the ever-growing spa and well-being industry.

This uniquely designed hotel and spa delves into the ancient cultures of Rajasthan, reproducing the vibrant, striking and surreal visual impact of 16th-century classical Mogul architecture. Inside you'll find plush furnishings, textiles, mosaics, paintings and carvings which took over 120 local artists and craftsmen to bring designer Stephen Hall's vision to fruition. The evocative silhouettes of the Islamic archways, the tastefully inlaid designs and the riot of colours used, such as gold, deep red and orange, contribute to the Mogul-like luxury.

THIS PAGE AND OPPOSITE:
Prana Spa is an imposing tribute to 16th-century Mogul architecture.

The jewel in this crown is Prana Spa, a sprawling 1,300 sq m (1,555 sq yd) complex offering an extensive range of spa treatments. Built in the breathtaking style of a luxurious Rajasthani palace, the spa has a vibrant facade that matches the ethnic furnishings inside. In fact, the interior is such a visual treat that Australian artist and entrepreneur Jim Elliot, who conceived this idea, calls an experience here 'part theatre and part therapy'. To enhance the authentic look and feel of the spa, the design team travelled to Rajasthan to hand-pick many of the spa's furnishings, including carpets, brass lanterns and silk paintings.

The magnificent stable of treatment rooms includes 24 massage rooms, one hot and two cold plunge pools, four rain shower massage rooms, two saunas and three steam rooms. Separates areas exist for reflexology and beauty treatments.

Prana Spa has over 70 spa therapists who hold international qualifications in their areas of specialisation, and they usually meditate before each treatment session. Besides helping them focus their talents and healing energies better, this practice underscores the vital significance of their vocation, which is sharing the gift of health. The meditative sounds and healing scents all around also contribute to helping guests achieve a very deep level of relaxation, so that both your body and mind leave each session with a sensation of utter bliss.

The menu of available services includes Ayurvedic treatments which use oils and powders imported from India, Indonesian beauty treatments such as the Boreh or Lulur body scrub, Russian therapeutic massage, barefoot Shiatsu massage and hydrotherapy sessions. A speciality here, however, is Prana Shirodara, a 60-minute Ayurvedic treament that begins with a soothing Indian head, scalp, neck and shoulder massage, followed by a more precise massage of the vital marma points to stimulate and energise the body. Warm, medicated oils will also be drizzled over the centre of your forehead

THIS PAGE (FROM TOP): Bedrooms feature the same vibrant mix of colours and textures visible elsewhere on the property; private pools and gardens are a feature of every villa

OPPOSITE: The evocative designs of the treatment rooms at Prana Spa appeal to your senses as much as the treatments do themselves.

for 20 minutes. This session is recommended for those with low energy levels, or those suffering from insomnia, chronic headaches, fatigue and stress in particular.

Completing the spa experience is The Restaurant at Prana. Here, guests will feast on spa cuisine prepared with organically grown produce, including salads prepared with special herbal ingredients. Cleansing drinks are an important part of the menu as well and aid detoxification. Those who long

for more conventional meals, however, will not go hungry as the restaurant offers international and traditional Balinese dishes too. An extensive room service menu is also available, serving a variety of Asian, Indonesian and Western food.

When it comes to accommodation and facilities, the hotel functions with all the hospitality and amenities of a five-star hotel. Each of the 50 private villas offers privacy and luxury, with high walls guaranteed to hold the outside world at bay. Choose from villas of varying sizes with one, two or three bedrooms, though all of them have equally luxurious facilities. Every villa comes with a private pool, landscaped garden and fully-equipped kitchen. The three-bedroom villas enjoy a slightly different set-up, with the third bedroom located in a separate circular villa just across the garden from the other two bedrooms. All three rooms, however, have

equal access to the swimming pool and other private areas. Although the villas feature traditional Balinese architecture, the interiors still have touches of vibrant colour reminiscent of the grandeur of Prana Spa, lying just outside their villas. This remarkable contrast ensures that your senses are enlivened the most when at Prana, and not when you're trying to unwind in your villa.

So, if you want a spa-focused holiday, The Villas Bali Hotel and Spa is definitely one of the better choices on the island.

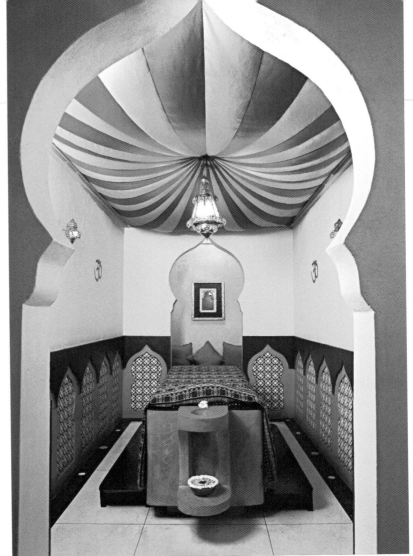

FACTS

ROOMS	16 one-bedroom villas • 7 two-bedroom villas • 25 three-bedroom villas
FOOD	The Restaurant at Prana: spa, international and Balinese
DRINK	maxi-bar
FEATURES	Prana Spa • private pool • fully-equipped private kitchen • complimentary shuttle bus service to Kuta
NEARBY	nightclubs • restaurants • temples
CONTACT	Jalan Kunti 118 X, Seminyak 80361 • telephone: +62.361.730 840 • facsimile: +62.361.733 751 • email: bookings@thevillas.net • website: www.thevillas.net

PHOTOGRAPHS COURTESY OF THE VILLAS BALI HOTEL AND SPA.

Waka Gangga

Most seaside resorts are restful, idyllic places that encourage you to unwind and let your worries slide. Waka Gangga, located in Tabanan, is one such resort, but with a little twist. Even though it has the Indian Ocean roaring right at its doorstep, guests are warned not to take their chances in the water on account of the mighty rip tides and undertows. What you can safely look forward to, however, is a string of evenings spent sipping a cocktail beside the pool, marvelling at how the fates conspired to bring you here, while the sun takes a bow beyond the distant waters.

THIS PAGE (CLOCKWISE FROM RIGHT):
Savour your meals at the edge of the Indian Ocean; a room with a view adds to the charm of this resort; surrounding rice fields convey a sense of earthy abundance.

OPPOSITE: Waka Gangga's architecture blends in perfectly with its rustic surroundings.

The structure that first catches your eye at Waka Gangga is definitely the large, round pavilion with a thatched roof, on an elevated bed of volcanic rock. This is the resort's dining room and it gets its inspiration from ancient Balinese castle battlements. The resort's general style, however, remains true to other Waka properties, faithfully replicating the agrarian-chic aesthetic that fits in perfectly with the verdant rice terraces on the other side of the resort.

Ten bungalows and a black-sand beach fronting the Indian Ocean form the rest of this cosy property. The villas are located on rice terraces leading down to the beach, with two villas per terrace. Inside the villas, stark but elegant furnishings based on Waka's essential triumvirate of bamboo, stone and thatch reflect a rustic sensibility and reinforce the awareness that you're not just far away from home, but also a world away from the urban grind. Here, within the comfortable confines of Waka Gangga,

guests are reminded of the more important things in life: quality time with your loved ones, and enjoying life's little pleasures, from the colours that fill your surroundings, to the feel of warm sand under your feet and between your toes.

To keep you happily occupied at Waka Gangga, there's a freshwater swimming pool for leisurely afternoon dips, and a spa with a jacuzzi and sauna to rejuvenate your senses. Day tours, including treks through the rice fields and visits to Tanah Lot, will also help you while away the hours.

Still, little else beats the exhilaration of a heart-thumping horseback ride up and down the inviting stretch of beach, especially as the sun sets. The local stables will set you up with all you need.

So, if you're looking for the kind of holiday that involves doing not much more than enjoying the sun, the sea and perhaps even the surf, Waka Gangga could just be the right choice for you.

PHOTOGRAPHS COURTESY OF WAKA GANGGA.

FACTS

ROOMS	10 bungalows
FOOD	restaurant: Balinese, Indonesian and Western
DRINK	bar
FEATURES	pool • spa • horseback riding • complimentary sunset cocktails
NEARBY	Tanah Lot • Yeh Gangga
CONTACT	Banjar Yeh Gangga, Desa Sudimara, Tabanan 82123 • telephone: +62.361.416 256 • facsimile: +62.361.416 353 • email: wakagangga@wakaexperience.com • website: www.wakaexperience.com

Tirtha Uluwatu

THIS PAGE AND OPPOSITE: **The striking wedding atrium floats on a shimmering pond and overlooks the Indian Ocean.**

When planning a wedding that's truly out of this world, the first item on your checklist would be hunting down a suitable location. For those who know and love Bali, there's one particular venue that quickly springs to mind: Tirtha Uluwatu. The word 'tirtha' in ancient Sanskrit translates as 'holy water'. Water not only performs an essential ceremonial function in traditional Hindu weddings, but also signifies the spiritual essence that all matter originates from. These uplifting themes of love and life-affirmation are appropriately reflected in the beautiful architecture and décor of this venue, located just a short walk away from the revered Pura Uluwatu temple in Bali's south.

There is no other place on the island so wholeheartedly devoted to bringing out the magic and romance of a tropical wedding. The interior design, bridal packages and even the custom programmes have been drawn up to fulfil every possible wedding fantasy. Couples are also assured of service so personalised that a dedicated wedding planner will always be on hand to help you glide through this most special occasion with nothing less than absolute peace of mind, knowing all your needs will be met.

The period of preparation begins with a warm welcome and a ferried ride from your hotel to the venue where the wedding package begins to unfold. Organising pre-nuptial essentials is a breeze thanks to the on-site bridal boutique, gift shop and wedding studio that co-ordinates both your photography and videography needs. The packages are styled to suit both Asian and Western preferences, but can also offer a creative fusion of both worlds. Couples are entertained in Tirtha's day suites while preparations for the event are underway. The day suites offer romantic views of the gardens, ocean and private pool, adding to the air of celebratory anticipation.

Following a brief meeting in Tirtha's reception lounge, the bride and groom are ushered over an elevated walkway and into the stylish and modern wedding atrium. Here, you'll find an altar constructed from delicate mother-of-pearl stands resting on a

sturdy bamboo base. The atrium itself is a dazzling A-line construction of white steel, glass and triangular sails. The solemnity and grandeur of the occasion is heightened by a procession of pageboys bearing Balinese ceremonial umbrellas and flower girls in their traditional dresses, while 'live' traditional Balinese music or a mellow violin duet play in the background. This culminates in the presentation of a certificate marking the couple's commitment and sealing the union.

Afterwards, the wedding party adjourns to the dining room where post-ceremony

festivities need not be anything less than explosive thanks to Tirtha's ready access to Bali's community of wedding event organisers, entertainers and performers. This room features a mix of teak and Chinese silk, with table settings that include exquisite china, crystalware, silverware, seashell vases, scented candles and generous floral arrangements to brighten up the place. A gourmet dinner—think Asian- and French-inspired dishes such as Hot and Spicy Asian Soup, Beef Bourgignon and Baked Valrhona Chocolate Tart Soufflé—is served behind

THIS PAGE (CLOCKWISE FROM RIGHT):
Enjoy a gourmet dinner in the
glass-panelled dining room;
architect Glenn Parker blended
Eastern minimalism with
contemporary tropical design to
create the wedding atrium.

OPPOSITE: The couple and their
guests enter the wedding atrium
via a floating walkway.

floor-to-ceiling windows that offer views of the landscaped gardens and the Indian Ocean stretching out across the horizon. Couples can also choose to hold the festivities in a more relaxed open-air pavilion where the wedding party can enjoy dinner and dancing under the night sky.

Credit for the tasteful, Asian minimalist look of the venue goes to interior designer Ratina Moegiono and landscape artist Made Wijaya, whose collaboration has resulted in a seamless and understated elegance. This is expressed through the use of comforting earth tones such as ochre, green and brown which are visually harmonised with outdoor sculptures by Made Cangker and Dewa Japa to inspire serenity. The setting is further accentuated by an abundance of flowers which lend both delicate colour and scent to every wedding. Besides bouquets and corsages, the chapel itself is decked with lovely fresh flowers such as orchids and assorted tropical blooms, while a generous shower of scented petals mark the end of the ceremony.

Sure enough, it is not just lovebirds who journey here, but many leading magazine photographers too. The numerous wedding-themed magazine features regularly styled and shot here have made quick fans of readers all around the world, to the extent that engagement parties, cocktail functions, corporate events or a quick mid-year sojourn are good enough reasons to head to Tirtha.

Do keep in mind, however, that Bali's dry seasons—April to June, and September to November—are the best time to fix a date here as these periods will ensure you leave with the most picturesque wedding photographs. Just imagine skies that are a deep blue, sunsets that leave comforting hues of orange, pink and purple, and a glistening Indian Ocean, against which your loved ones in all their wedding finery will be beautifully framed.

PHOTOGRAPHS COURTESY OF TIRTHA ULUWATU.

FACTS		
ROOMS	1 wedding atrium • 3 private dining rooms • 5 day suites • 1 open-air dining pavilion	
FOOD	Asian and French	
DRINK	liquor and wines	
FEATURES	outdoor dance floor • guest club lounge and deck • wedding boutique • café • florist	
NEARBY	Pura Uluwatu • Nusa Dua	
CONTACT	Jalan Raya Uluwatu, Banjar Karang Boma, Uluwatu 80361 • telephone: +62.361.772 255 • facsimile: +62.361.777 252 • email: wedding-coordinator@tirthabali.com • website: www.tirthabali.com	

Henna Spa at Villa Balquisse

Set delightfully close to the rustic fishing village of Jimbaran in south Bali, Henna Spa is a charming facility located within the beautiful surrounds of Villa Balquisse. Those seeking solitude at this tranquil and enriching destination will not only depart truly satisfied, but will take away images and memories that will last a lifetime.

The menu of exclusive services includes an array of massage and beauty treatments, a relaxing flower bath and much more. The two private massage rooms were designed to harmonise with the look of the main villa. Both rooms feature Colonial-style interiors accentuated with Javanese touches. In these stylish rooms, guests can enjoy the Javanese Lulur Royal Ritual, an elaborate treatment given to the royal brides of Yogyakarta during the Majapahit era just before the ceremony, and the Balinese Boreh Royal Ritual, which utilises a traditional body scrub recipe popularly used on the island.

The spa's signature offerings include the aromatic Balinese Coffee Body Scrub—highly recommended for men—which seeks to energise the body and guide your physical, mental and spiritual states toward health and harmony; the Volcanic Clay

THIS PAGE (CLOCKWISE FROM RIGHT): A pond flows around and under the spa facility; the collection of antiques and antique reproductions lend the place a vintage charm; handcrafted ornaments and beautiful fabrics reflect the owners' discerning tastes.

OPPOSITE (FROM LEFT): Enjoy a leisurely soak in an outdoor bath; therapists skilled in traditional treatments massage away your woes.

...Henna Spa is a charming facility located within the beautiful surrounds of Villa Balquisse.

Body Scrub which exfoliates dead skin cells and soothes the epidermis while the gentle pressure applied by the therapist works to relieve tension, leaving you feeling relaxed; and the classic reflexology package which targets reflex points on the feet to stimulate and improve circulation around the main glands and organs throughout the body.

Given that massage treatments are indeed a widespread practice in Indonesia, Henna Spa also offers specially customised massages for children. Just as Indonesian infants are regularly massaged to aid the development of strong bones and muscles, and also to help them fall into sound and uninterrupted sleep at night, visiting children under the age of 12 can now experience this gentle and comforting treatment and learn to appreciate the benefits of caring for their bodies at an early age. In addition, parents get to enjoy some quality time together while the kids are occupied.

With easy access to an emerald coloured swimming pool, and the beach just 300 m (984 ft) away, guests will have endless opportunities to unwind outdoors in the sun as well. And when mealtime arrives, the obliging kitchen staff can also be counted on to serve healthy food in delicious variations. In this way, Henna Spa serves to nourish you inside and out.

More than just a place where relaxing treatments are administered, Henna Spa at Villa Balquisse provides a broader and more holistic retreat experience.

FACTS		
TREATMENTS	massages • body scrubs and wraps • flower baths	
FOOD	Banyan Restaurant: spa and fusion	
DRINK	restaurant bar	
FEATURES	pool • massages for children	
NEARBY	fishing village	
CONTACT	Jalan Uluwatu 18X, Jimbaran 80361 • telephone: +62.361.701 695 • facsimile: +62.361.701 695 • email: info@balquisse.com • website: www.balquisse.com	

PHOTOGRAPHS COURTESY OF RICHARD WATSON.

Hu'u Bar

Not too long ago, Hu'u Bar occupied a particularly hip and artistic corner of the Singapore Art Museum. And just as it used to dish out chic doses of acid jazz escapism to an appreciative downtown crowd every night in Singapore, Hu'u has taken shape in Bali as a similarly trendy spot with good food and a groove that sets it ahead of the pack. Still, the urban-chic theme has undergone a change: settling down on Jalan Petitenget, Hu'u Bar is now a restaurant, bar, lounge and club occupying 20,000 sq m (23,920 sq yd). It even has a swimming pool on the premises so guests can spend a whole day lazing around and getting a tan before partying the night away.

Fancy a little poolside celebration with some gourmet seafood? A couple of happy hour cocktails with new business associates to better seal the deal? Or just plagued by cravings for a sinful dessert while listening to hip sounds from a host of international DJs? Hu'u Bar accommodates all these desires and more with a busy schedule of parties and events, and a style that's hard to beat.

The interior here is a glamorous blend of Zen minimalism with hints of Balinese and ethnic Asian influences. This goes well with the venue's hip, unabashedly cosmopolitan vibe, a concept that is perfectly juxtaposed against the sunny skies and sandy shores of Petitenget Beach. The open, spacious

...a glamorous blend of Zen minimalism with hints of Balinese and ethnic Asian influences.

design lets cool breezes drift through, reminding guests of their proximity to the ocean and enhancing the holiday mood.

Music is certainly a draw here, with international DJs routinely flown in to man the mixing deck. Armed with their own prized records, these maestros can instantly transform the overall vibe of the venue with their sets. The broad spectrum of acid jazz and improvisationary grooves remain hot favourites with the crowd, while the more abstract and challenging electronic tunes take a while to get under your skin, but in time, you'll find yourself moving along to the beat as well. Occasionally, Hu'u Bar plays host to world artistes who perform in the tropical garden while guests lounge about on comfortable sofas and arm chairs.

THIS PAGE AND OPPOSITE: *Much more than a casual club, Hu'u Bar's fine interior décor appeals to a sophisticated and cosmopolitan crowd.*

The drive to innovate extends to the kitchen, where eclectic international dishes are concocted with fresh produce including organic vegetables sourced from Bali's Bedugul highlands. Among the highly recommended starters are the Deep-Fried Calamari, cooked with flour and herbs and served with a dash of tartar sauce, the Roast Duck Pancake Crepês with cucumber, and the Chicken Yakitori, marinated and grilled to its tasty best. The hearty selection of soups includes seafood favourites such as the Lemon Grass and Tamarind Broth with Baby Lobster, Sea Scallops and Mussels, the Fish

Consommé, a double-boiled clear fish soup with lobster dumplings and vegetables, and Soto Ayam, a traditional Indonesian clear chicken soup with glass noodles and bean sprouts. As for the selection of main courses, the Rack of Lamb served with rosemary sauce and Hu'u mash potatoes, and the Grilled Marinated Tofu served with roasted capsicum, soya butter and jasmine rice, are popular choices with diners.

The crowd is no less discerning when it comes to the sweet stuff. From the dessert menu, choose tempting creations such as the Valrhona White and Dark Chocolate Mousse, Hu'u Apple Pie with a scoop of vanilla ice cream, and Strawberry Sago, also served with vanilla ice cream.

Cocktails are a speciality here, with a range of over 70 concoctions including the popular Lychee Martini, Hu'u Absolut Martini and the Absolut Massive Attack.

THIS PAGE (FROM TOP): Asian specialities are prepared with fresh ingredients and organic produce; the chic dining area is perfect for intimate dinners and large gatherings.

OPPOSITE: Make yourself at home on a couch or bar stool and enjoy a few of Hu'u Bar's refreshing cocktails.

Other intriguing choices include the Cookie Monster (a warm mix of Bailey's Irish Cream, Kahlua, milk and Oreo cookies), the Zombie Hu'udini (gold and white rum flavoured with orange and lime juice), and the Screaming Orgasm (Bailey's Irish Cream, Cointreau, milk, and just as importantly, a sense of humour). A selection of fresh fruit Daiquiries and over 40 wine and Champagne labels from both the Old World and New World ensure you won't be left wanting.

The entire Hu'u vision is expressed so powerfully that regular patrons even respond instinctively by dressing up to complement the establishment's visual style, reflecting the same colours, textures and cuts.

Named after a small atoll off the island of Sumbawa—recognised for some of the best waves in the world—Hu'u expresses an international style that encapsulates the best of both the East and the West. This ensures all guests feel right at home here, no matter where they come from.

PHOTOGRAPHS COURTESY OF HU'U BAR.

FACTS

SEATS	70	
FOOD	international	
DRINK	lounge • bar	
FEATURES	pool • organic produce • dance floor • guest DJs • speciality cocktails	
NEARBY	Petitenget Beach • shops • cafés	
CONTACT	No. 1 Gang Gagak, Jalan Petitengget, Kerobokan, Kuta 80361 • telephone: +62.361.736 443 • facsimile: +62.361.736 573 • email: huubali@indo.net.id • website: www.huubali.com	

Kafe Warisan

Whether you're here for a leisurely meal in the spacious garden, a romantic evening for two on the terrace, or a quick drink or two with your travel companions by the bar, Kafe Warisan, a French-Mediterranean restaurant in Seminyak, has been known to cast its trendy spell on one and all.

As befits a fine dining establishment, the restaurant lives up to its reputation by maintaining a sophisticated menu and an experienced staff who extend a gracious welcome and provide excellent service. Perhaps the most memorable element of the Kafe Warisan experience, however, is the air of creativity that pervades and finds expression not only in the food, but in the captivating works of art on display.

The signature menu was conceptualised to express the culinary credo that one should not merely eat to live, but live to eat, and with great gusto too. The restaurant has earned its superlative standing through the dedicated efforts and creative passions of French partners Said Alem and Nicolas Tourneville, who launched Kafe Warisan in 1997 with the self-imposed charter of

...one should not merely eat to live, but live to eat, and with great gusto too.

raising the quality of dining experiences in Bali to the highest standard they could.

Chef Nicolas seems to have a natural talent for reconfiguring a three-course lunch or dinner menu into a truly gastronomical experience that begs a lingering glass of wine or a cigar at the end, just to prolong the experience. Reviewers seldom fail to acknowledge his genius, and even marvel with some degree of wonder, at how he draws inspiration from Bali's local markets, browsing the seasonal produce and fresh ingredients to elicit novel ideas, and the way he infuses his creations with a personal energy that is delightful on the palate but hard to pin down in words.

On the plate, though, Chef Nicolas's signature touch is brilliantly translated via favourites like the Crab Bisque and the Grilled Scallops and Prawns. Given the wide range of desirable dishes here, even the more regular patrons find it difficult to reduce the menu to just a few favourites. Those who enjoy culinary pleasures in a set package might opt for the Romantic Dinner Menu which seeks to satisfy both the stomach and the heart. This menu includes the Trio Carpaccio with Red Capsicum Coulis and Spices, Hot Foie Gras with Clear Miso Soup, Pan-Roasted Salmon and Asparagus Saffron Risotto, Grilled Duck Breast with Potato Gnocchi and Cabernet

THIS PAGE: Kafe Warisan's experienced bartenders will be pleased to serve you a Cuban cigar or a refreshing cocktail.

OPPOSITE (FROM TOP) Chef Nicolas is responsible for the array of dishes that inspire guests to want a little bit of everything; evenings at Kafe Warisan are a lively event.

THIS PAGE: *Verdant rice fields come right up to the restaurant's border.*

OPPOSITE (CLOCKWISE FROM LEFT): *Rustic sophistication best describes the style here; Chef Nicolas's inventive menu is as much a visual treat as it is tantalising to the palate.*

baby vegetables and chick peas, or the Pan-Roasted Alaskan Cod Fish with capers and asparagus, for a hearty main course; and something sweet and surprising from the dessert menu like the raspberry soufflé.

Kafe Warisan's popularity and exclusive status is the reason why guests need to call in advance for a reservation or make a booking via email. For your efforts, a leaf might be painted with your name on it and placed on the table to acknowledge the thoughtful reservation. Once successful in securing a place for your dinner party, you then have a choice of occupying one of four dining areas—the Upper Galleries, the Garden and Lower Gallery, the Rice Field Patio or the Bar—each adding its distinct character to your dining experience.

Dining on the first floor is particularly memorable as guests will enjoy views of the garden and expansive rice fields. It is also here that some of the more talented artists in Bali routinely display their artworks for your viewing pleasure. The garden, covered gallery and bar are also lovely places to dine, especially in the evening when the area is illuminated with candles, adding a touch of romance that complements the rustic surroundings perfectly.

Should the need for an especially intimate occasion arise, guests can request a table in the Rice Field Patio. This covered

Reduction, and a Hot Chocolate Soufflé in unhurried succession. Otherwise, taking a chance on something new and unfamiliar will yield just as rewarding an experience.

Though the menu is refreshed regularly, notable dishes to look out for include the Warm Duck Salad accompanied by basilic mango coulis, or the Roasted Mushrooms stuffed with escargot, for their rich flavours; the Seven Hours Lamb Shoulder served with

...taking a chance on something new and unfamiliar will yield just as rewarding an experience.

area is set with tables for two and offers a little more privacy. Here, guests will surely enjoy sampling a good selection from Kafe Warisan's extensive list of French, Australian and Californian wines, with the sounds of light jazz filtering through the air, and a flurry of stars lighting up the night sky. And besides a cocktail or preferred beer of your choice, there's also the extravagance of a Cuban cigar and Cognac to look forward to. What better way could there be to enjoy a tropical evening in paradise?

FACTS

SEATS	Upper Galleries: 85 • Garden and Lower Gallery: 80 • Rice Field Patio: 20
FOOD	French-Mediterranean
DRINK	bar
FEATURES	cigars • art displays • vegetarian selections
NEARBY	Warisan Gallery • Pura Petitenget
CONTACT	No. 38 Jalan Raya Kerobokan, Banjar Taman, Kuta 80361 • telephone: +62.361.731 175 • facsimile: +62.361.732 762 • email: info@kafewarisan.com • website: www.kafewarisan.com

PHOTOGRAPHS COURTESY OF KAFE WARISAN.

Khaima Restaurant

Khaima Restaurant is Bali's first restaurant serving Moroccan cuisine. This place enjoys a steady crowd of regulars and first-timers alike, keen to partake in an engaging dining experience. In fact, diners should make reservations well in advance to avoid disappointment. It is not just the restaurant's authentic cuisine, prepared by chef Nora Tabakalt, that excites the imagination. The interior too, designed by Zohra Boukhari, is thoroughly inviting and exotic, with an Arabian theme that evokes a sense of adventure and discovery.

It is revealing that 'khaima' is Arabic for 'tent', and the name fits well. Not only do diners first have to step through the flaps of a tent to enter the main dining area, the garden at the back is also sheltered under a tent or marquee, with tables strategically arranged around a lovely central water fountain. A number of fans keep a gentle and comfortable breeze wafting through the space. The decision to do away with the more conventional enclosed and air-conditioned interior has ensured that the old-world ambience is maintained. These features endow the restaurant with an air of intrigue, fantasy and glamour, and diners tend to feel like they're stepping into an old Hollywood movie set. As part of the delightful illusion, the staff are dressed in traditional Moroccan attire with baggy

...Bali's first restaurant serving Moroccan cuisine.

trousers, slippers and turbans. To top this off, belly dancers perform every Friday and Saturday night to the delight of diners.

An extensive menu is available for lunch and dinner, though the selection in the afternoon is smaller. For a light lunch, order the salads which are prepared with simple greens but dressed with unexpected spicy flavourings. The Cinnamon Carrot Salad (Schlada Bal Khizou Wa Farfa) stands out for its unusual mix of ingredients and textures, while the Chachouka consists of tomatoes and bell peppers tossed together and warmed just enough to bring out their respective flavours. Equally rewarding are the Eggplant Salad, and the Mechouia, a skewered serving of green peppers.

Both the vegetable-based Chorba soup and the spicy Baissar (a type of lentil soup) are hearty and satisfying, especially with some Khobz Ed Dar, a popular traditional Moroccan bread which is available plain or with sesame seeds. This can be followed by savoury Moroccan pastries known as Briouats which come with a variety of spicy fillings. A highlight is the mixed plate of three pastries stuffed with minced beef, shredded chicken and goat cheese. Alternatively, diners can select individual pastries and fillings, with the more popular variations featuring either tuna in olive oil (Briouats Bal Tun), saffron chicken (Briouats

THIS PAGE (FROM TOP): **A water fountain takes pride of place in the dining tent; sit back, relax and take a few puffs from a traditional hookah.**
OPPOSITE: **Vibrant colours reflect Moroccan influences and add to the festive atmosphere.**

Bal Djaje), goat cheese (Briouats Bal Jben), or vegetables (Briouats Bal Balkhodra).

The selection of main courses feature a choice of three distinct dishes: Tagines (meat stewed in a special ceramic pot shaped like a cone), Kaskous (or couscous) and Mechoui (grilled and skewered meat). The Lamb Tagines are particularly delicious and are served with vegetables and warm Moroccan bread to ensure the gravy does not go to waste. The Tagine Bal Ghalmi Wa Danjale, or Lamb and Eggplant Tagine, is just as hearty and mouth-watering—the seasoned meat oozing with tasty juices.

Highlights from the Kaskous selection include the Kaskous Tfaya, lamb flavoured with onions and raisins; Kaskou Bal Ghalmi Mechoui, essentially a lamb kebab; Kaskous Bal Khodra, a combination of vegetables; and the ever-popular Kaskous Bal Merguez, which pairs mixed vegetables with some spicy merguez sausage.

Diners who would like to try traditional Moroccan grilled specialities can choose from Khaima's delicious chicken (Mechoui Bal Djaje), lamb (Mechoui Bal Ghalmi) and beef (Mechoui Bal Hjale) variations. These are also popular with diners.

THIS PAGE: *Enjoy a formal setting indoors or chill out al fresco in a cosy corner.*

OPPOSITE: *Intricately carved furnishings give diners more to appreciate than just the delectable food.*

Round off the meal with a sweet treat or two from the dessert menu. Try a slice of the rich almond and walnut cake prepared Arabian style, or a serving of orange salad with orange flower water for a tangy and refreshing end. If you're not too full, make it a point to sample the traditional almond milk, green mint tea or the superlatively rich Moroccan coffee. The distinctively novel flavours of these classic beverages will tease your tastebuds and impress upon you the signature flavours of Moroccan cuisine.

While lounging cross-legged on a generous pile of cushions later, enjoying those gently intoxicating puffs from the hookah on the floor, or just appreciating the rich aromas that fill the air, you'll know one thing for certain, Khaima Restaurant offers a truly memorable dining experience. Before you leave, remember to have your hands or feet decorated in swirling henna patterns by the in-house artist as a lovely memento of your visit here.

FACTS		
SEATS	inside: 62 • tent: 15
FOOD	Moroccan
DRINK	traditional Moroccan beverages • wine list
FEATURES	belly dance performances on Friday and Saturday nights
NEARBY	restaurants • cafés • shops
CONTACT	Jalan Laksmana, Seminyak 80361 • telephone: +62.361.742 3925 • facsimile: +62.361.738 627 • email: khaima@balquisse.com •

PHOTOGRAPHS COURTESY OF BLAISE SAMOY.

Ku Dé Ta

Ku Dé Ta, a beachfront restaurant in Seminyak, has made an inspired investment in modern architecture, classy interior design and an original menu, and this has paid off handsomely. Today, the restaurant attracts an ever-increasing community of enthusiastic patrons, all with the desire to experience Ku Dé Ta's exceptionally fine cuisine and enjoy the sophisticated company within its laid-back tropical surroundings.

Against the unmistakably Balinese backdrop of palm trees and the endless Indian Ocean, French architect Fredo Tafin's eye-catching structure exudes all the luxury and exclusivity of a private beach club in Europe. Whether you're lazing on a custom-made lounger by the white-sand beach, or simply waiting for the sun to oblige with a blazing sunset, there's no denying the draw of this five-star, resort-like restaurant, where

the staff regularly get asked, "So, where are the suites?", by appreciative guests.

In fact, it would be more appropriate to call Ku Dé Ta an entertainment venue rather than a restaurant because many guests come here to spend a day lazing on the beach, usually arriving in time for breakfast, later indulging in a sumptuous lunch, before

THIS PAGE (FROM TOP): Dine with the quintessential Balinese view of palm trees and the Indian Ocean ahead of you; chic and inviting on the inside, this restaurant is a popular spot with celebrities.

OPPOSITE: Striking red streamers flapping in the wind add to the party atmosphere.

cleaning themselves up in the evening and enjoying a leisurely dinner. After dinner, it is time to party to the sounds of visiting international DJs. This venue also regularly hosts private parties, cocktail gatherings and even the odd wedding. A full-time functions team is available to organise every detail, from the flowers to the decorations, the music and most importantly, the food. Many multinational corporations have held events here, including BMW, Cathay Pacific, Credit Suisse, Fashion TV and Singapore Airlines. With such prominent attention, it is no wonder Ku Dé Ta has warranted a mention in *The New York Times*.

Whether it's breakfast, lunch, dinner or supper, Australian chefs Asif Mehrudeen and Rob Staedler take pride in maintaining a menu that is thoroughly imaginative and flavoursome. The selection of international cuisine features simple but hearty seafood dishes including Linguine with Seafood tossed in aged Italian olive oil and dried chilli and lemon, Chilli-Salted Squid, Grilled Freshwater Prawns and Char Grilled 'Live' Rock Lobster. Most of the seafood is locally caught, thus ensuring it is as fresh as can be. Meat-lovers, have no fear because there's also the King Island Beef Carppacio served with baby capers, rucola and a Parmesan dressing, and the most extravagant 90-Day Aged Wagyu Sirloin with a pink peppercorn

separate building on the premises and has a number of good Cuban imports suitable for post-dinner appreciation. With a drink in one hand, a cigar in the other, and a catchy groove in your head, you'll be all set for a night spent partying on the beach until the wee hours of the morning.

Decked out in their stylish designer casuals—white linen beachwear for the more conservative, sarongs and bikinis for the less inhibited—and sporting a flawless tan, the merry-makers mingle patiently while the sun goes down and the DJ warms up, before letting loose and bringing down the house. Count on celebrity DJs, such as Claude Challe—previously with Paris's Budhha Bar—to oblige with a mix of house, ambient, tribal and down-tempo grooves.

THIS PAGE (FROM TOP): With excellent views, lots to do and great food, beachfront dining is even more appealing at Ku Dé Ta; besides the sumptuous menu, guests can also expect a visual treat while exploring the venue.
OPPOSITE: The lounge is perfect for mellow midday gatherings.

sauce. When it's time for a sweet treat, the delightful Valrhona Chocolate Pudding with homemade tangerine ice cream, or the Warm Tapioca Soup with fresh rambutans come highly recommended.

Ku Dé Ta does not fall short when it comes to drinks either. The venue has three bars housing a wide selection of wines from France, Italy, Australia, New Zealand and Chile, and a premium selection of ports, cognacs and liqueurs, best enjoyed with an extravagant cigar from Fidel's. This air-conditioned cigar lounge can be found in a

There's always a chance you might get carried away on your first visit, and before you know it, find yourself squinting at the rising sun the next morning. If that does happen, just rub the drowsiness from your eyes, adjourn to the deck and start ordering a scrumptious breakfast. Choose from a selection of fruit juices and smoothies to perk yourself up, then tuck into something utterly satisfying like the Poached Eggs with Portobello Mushrooms, Asparagus and Shaved Parmesan, or the filling Tasmanian Smoked Salmon Bagel with Lemon Cream Cheese. Remember to save some space for a tropical fruit salad and a foamy latte before hitting the road.

For the guys left to run the show here, things can only get bigger and better. The Ku Dé Ta formula works so well that there has already been talk of exporting it to some of the world's best beaches in Europe and Asia. Keep your eyes peeled because one might just turn up near you.

PHOTOGRAPHS COURTESY OF CHRISTOPHER LEGGETT.

FACTS		
	SEATS	200
	FOOD	modern international
	DRINK	3 bars
	FEATURES	beach • organic produce • cigar lounge • international DJs
	NEARBY	Seminyak • Kuta
	CONTACT	No. 9 Jalan Laksmana, Seminyak Beach 80361 • telephone: +62.361.736 969 • facsimile: +62.361.736 767 • email: info@kudeta.net • website: www.kudeta.net

Haveli

Haveli is a stylish and upmarket furnishings and linen gallery located in Seminyak. The store specialises in both traditional and contemporary designs that reflect a taste and appreciation for uniquely Oriental, Moroccan and Indian heritage. The name Haveli was taken from a legendary residence in Rajasthan, India, belonging to a prosperous merchant who made his livelihood along the legendary trade routes linking Iran, Afghanistan, India and China.

Haveli carries a wide selection of elegant and eye-catching items you might want to acquire for your home. Its in-store catalogue covers an extensive range of tableware, glassware, lighting, accessories and numerous linen products, with Oriental handicrafts and furniture being a highlight. These include handcrafted wooden tables, chairs, wardrobes and canopy bed frames, as well as smaller side pieces carved with authentic motifs and patterns. Collectors and interior designers alike will be thrilled to discover such exquisite finds in the aisles here, while trendy hotel decorators and home owners will surely gravitate towards the more distinctively earthy or ethnic pieces that effectively convey a natural or tribal feel. The glass creations displayed throughout the gallery are just as colourful and sophisticated, and have been moulded into unusual drinking vessels, storage jars

THIS PAGE (CLOCKWISE FROM RIGHT):
Simple yet distinctive metalwork is a favourite with customers worldwide; Haveli's rich fabrics can be combined and layered to create an extravagant look; an arrangement of cushions on a bed reflect the royal opulence of ancient India and the Middle East.

OPPOSITE: Haveli's collection is comprehensive, allowing shoppers to easily match a tableware set with all sorts of dining accessories.

candle holders and decorative vases. Clearly the product of fine materials and talented craftsmanship, these stunning items will endow any living or working space with a distinct look, and have, as a result, found their way into many homes and hotels.

Best of all, the showrooms here are designed such that shoppers can quickly pick out complete dining table sets or put together a coherent living room arrangement simply by viewing the wide selection of furnishings and accessories on display. To help shoppers visualise the total effect of combining the complementary pieces, many arrangements have been styled and assembled all around the store to inspire customers and emphasise the need for a strong, holistic focus when decorating.

The desire to inspire is enhanced by rows of exotic supplies such as pigments for colouring cement, all sorts of local spices, flavoured coffee and other items. Also available are numerous items of jewellery, elegantly crafted to complement a formal evening dress and accentuate the wearer's feminine flair. Indeed, as shoppers browse through the displays, the sheer variety of colours, textures and forms will surely draw out one enthusiastic response after another.

In particular, Haveli's linenware range is of such high repute and has grown so large that it is now marketed as the

THIS PAGE: *The use of strong, vibrant colours, even on something as simple as a cushion, can liven up a living space.*
OPPOSITE: *The displays in the store offer ideas and inspiration to shoppers.*

Shahinaz Collection. This line is managed and designed by Zohra Boukhari, an interior decorator and entrepreneur of Moroccan descent. In fact, the line shares its name with Zohra's second daughter, making it a very personal collection. The luxurious creations you will find carrying its stamp of approval include napkins, table sets, cushion covers, kimonos and bedlinen, all made from the finest Indonesian fabrics, in colours and patterns traditionally associated with local fashion. Contemporary designs abound as well, especially for sofa spreads, cushion covers, pillow cases, lamp shades and curtains. Many of these bear minimalist, handcrafted patterns rendered on quality materials, and in styles and colours carefully matched to express a very chic Oriental sensibility. The cool and comforting texture of linen is put to good use especially in the children's collection, with a range of bedlinen, crib sets and clothing to keep the little ones cool in the tropics.

Since its opening in 2002, the store has extended its expertise to handle lifestyle-oriented interior consulting, and also organises shopping excursions for foreign clients who wish to tour the various related boutiques, craft centres, warehouses and suppliers in the vicinity. This makes it easier for avid shoppers to buy exactly what they

want without much hassle. Haveli's keen interest in servicing customers from around the world shows in the comprehensive and thoughtful design solutions that are typically proposed, whether for business or home needs. This covers aspects ranging from the selection of materials, to custom designs and any export paperwork. In fact, Haveli's reputation and reach is so extensive that many of their major clients overseas look forward to receiving shipments on a regular basis throughout the year. These include hotels, resorts and homes worldwide. It is through these contacts that an increasing number of people have come to learn of, and appreciate, Haveli's products.

Today, with almost three-quarters of their stocks marked for customers and resellers internationally, the Haveli name has gained much respect as a global brand for Oriental and Indonesian furnishings and accessories. It has, indeed, become a brand which customers can count on.

PHOTOGRAPHS COURTESY OF HAVELI.

FACTS

PRODUCT	tableware • bedlinen • glassware • lighting • linen products • jewellery • outdoor and indoor furniture
FEATURES	Oriental furniture and furnishings • Shahinaz Collection • children's range • handcrafted and machine-produced items
NEARBY	restaurants • cafés • shops
CONTACT	Nos. 15 and 38 Jalan Basangkasa, Seminyak 80361 • telephone: +62.361.737 160 • facsimile: +62.361.724 497 • email: haveli@equinoxtrading.com • website: www.equinoxtrading.com

Jenggala Keramik Bali

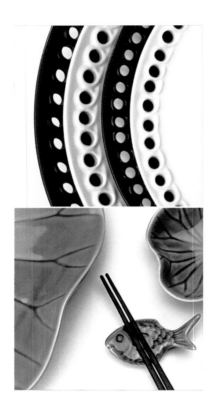

Founded in 1976, Jenggala Keramik Bali is an inspired, cross-cultural collaboration between the late designer and potter Brent Hesselyn from New Zealand, the late Indonesian hotelier Wija Waworuntu, and the latter's daughter, Ade. From their modest workshop in Batu Jimbar, Sanur, they made a passionate effort to present the native crafts of Bali to a growing market of ethnic art collectors around the world and the local hospitality market. This venture quickly started gaining a loyal base of customers through a focus on quality craftsmanship and contemporary modifications to traditional styles. Jenggala Keramik has since become a leading global producer of ceramic, glass and table-top accessories. The company is recognised for its chic designs, innovative use of materials, and skilful artisans who continue to push stylistic boundaries.

Now based in Jimbaran, the company is still wooing a large international market with its constant flow of fresh ideas. Following Brent Hesselyn's original concept and design base, Jenggala meets with clients from various markets and turns their decorative dreams into reality with brilliant customised solutions. Their handcrafted products have

THIS PAGE: Jenggala Keramik's ceramic products incorporate an extensive range of colours and surface finishes, with forms that are clean, cool and simply elegant.

OPPOSITE (FROM TOP): Jenggala's headquarters in southern Bali feature extensive facilities; stylised bowls feature the Balinese Cili design, the inspiration for Jenggala's logo.

a distinctive look and feel: while the clean lines express a contemporary focus on elegance and visual economy, the physical shapes themselves are strongly influenced by symbols of nature, particularly those of Bali, and dominate a large number of ethnic Asian art forms and collections.

Jenggala Keramik's supporting operations include a production facility, an expansive retail showroom, a café and an exhibition gallery dedicated to showcasing the works of both Indonesian and international artists.

Every month the commissioned output includes stoneware and porcelain ceramics, hand-blown and slumped glass products,

and many new designs making their debut as well. The ceramics line is especially noteworthy because it is produced on a made-to-order basis from a catalogue that spans over 2,500 designs and 100 types of glaze finishes. The glazes and clay bodies used are made with proprietary processes developed and perfected by Jenggala since its founding. These processes involve the innovative fusion of materials, resulting in surprising surfaces, unique finishes and, most recently, a ceramic product that is vitrified and chip resistant. Such a strategy ensures that every piece made by Jenggala is actually tailored to the

THIS PAGE (CLOCKWISE FROM TOP):
The Nautilus shell inspired these elegant designs; satin white, Jenggala's most popular finish, and satin vibrant blue add a light touch to any table setting; intriguing items such as this Dewi Sri-style salt and pepper holder are a Jenggala original.

OPPOSITE: *The Nori collection has a contemporary look that combines geometric shapes with subtle lines and soft edges in ceramic and complementary glass designs.*

particular space and use it is meant for, and optimises its contribution to setting the mood.

Jenggala's glass artist-in-residence is Richard Morrell, an established name in the Australian glass art scene with a creative career that spans more than 20 years. International talents who regularly contribute to the company's collections come from a variety of sources including an in-house design team, a visiting artist programme and consultants such as Masayo Tokumaru—a designer and stylist based in Japan who has been producing her own range in collaboration with Jenggala for many years.

The company's Jimbaran facility offers a stimulating platform for artistic dialogue and discovery. Jenggala's artisans actively engage visiting artists in discussions and demonstrations about new techniques and approaches relevant to their respective fields. This results in a constantly evolving collection that is imaginatively tailored to suit modern homes, restaurants, hotels and other spaces. Jenggala's artisans also keep up to date on the very latest technologies and production methods, thus remaining highly innovative with design details and the application of decorative finishes.

This same creative spirit has extended to the café adjoining the exhibition gallery and demonstration area which serves as

an interactive centre for sharing ideas over a light meal and a freshly brewed cup of coffee or tea. Taking this interactivity further, Jenggala's Paint-a-Pot facility catches budding artists and craftsmen at a tender age and invites the young and the young-at-heart to try their hand at painting ceramic items with brushes and stencils. As messy and uneven as the initial attempts might be, the participants tend to come away with a heightened appreciation for the crafts that Jenggala Keramik specialise in, and a life-long passion for these art forms.

Along with these workshops, Jenggala offers ceramic pottery courses for children and adults on a regular basis. These classes should be booked in advance and are open to individuals and groups. For a small fee, get your work fired in Jenggala's kilns. Whether it is a mug, plate, vase, teapot, decorative dish or Valentine's Day heart, the end result can be used as a personalised gift, like no other souvenir or memento can.

FACTS

PRODUCTS	ceramic and glass table-top accessories • table settings
FEATURES	customised designs • exhibition gallery • retail outlet • café • interactive programmes
NEARBY	Jimbaran Bay • Pura Uluwatu • Jimbaran Market
CONTACT	Jalan Uluwatu II, Jimbaran 80361 • telephone: +62.361.703 311 • facsimile: +62.361.703 312 • email: info@jenggala-bali.com • website: www.jenggala-bali.com

PHOTOGRAPHS COURTESY OF JENGGALA KERAMIK BALI.

Uluwatu Handmade Balinese Lace

Modern style, outstanding workmanship, a traditional spirit and classic comfort: these qualities are but the tip of the iceberg when contemplating the various reasons why Uluwatu Handmade Balinese Lace remains so popular with visitors to the island.

A home-grown garment manufacturer with its own retail chain, this boutique lace-maker uses a technique internationally known as cutwork, or krawang in Bahasa Indonesia. As with most authentic Balinese crafts, Uluwatu's cutwork is still made the traditional way with foot-powered machines many consider relics of a bygone era.

When talented Balinese women tested their traditional craft skills on lace back in the 1930s, they mastered techniques which were quickly disappearing around the world. This technique, used by Uluwatu, involves stretching the fabric over bamboo hoops which move back and forth with expert precision, allowing the thread to build layer upon successive layer. The final result is a labour of love and a work of art, as it is a single dedicated craftsperson who sees the process to completion. Just one item can take five or more days to complete.

In comparison, lace made from an electric machine is generally less durable because the even weave produced is not as interlocked. As a result, a single, broken thread can cause a whole section to

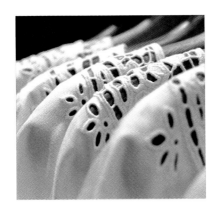

Uluwatu then turned its attention to creating new and contemporary designs backed by an unwavering focus on using quality fabrics and traditional craftsmanship.

Thus prompted by circumstance, Made embraced a more mature vision for her company and boldly realigned the business to take on the boutique market. Uluwatu launched a new range of ladies' fashion

THIS PAGE *(FROM TOP): The detailing on Uluwatu's lace tops showcase the quality handiwork you can expect from all their products; bedlinen is a favourite with discerning shoppers.*
OPPOSITE: *The boutiques offer nothing less than a stylish and sophisticated shopping experience.*

unravel. Handmade lace, though uneven, is considered special simply because the buyer is aware of the time and effort put into creating such pieces.

Established in the early 1980s, Uluwatu is a product of the youthful enthusiasm of Made Djati, then a 17-year-old girl from Kuta who was fascinated with the brightly-coloured lace wear favoured by the era's surfer girls. The fledgling company took its name from the legendary temple Pura Uluwatu, located on a cliff above the Indian Ocean, an area that was swiftly gaining international renown as a surfer's paradise. The temple is also of personal significance because Made's family counts among the thousands that make the pilgrimage there annually to mark the temple's anniversary.

As it often happens with fashion, however, the colourful and fun surfer girl look lost its mass appeal in the mid-1980s.

and accessories including a line of clothing (nightwear too), sashes, bags, bedlinen, table linen, hair bands, scarves, and more, targeted at the sophisticated woman. The success of Uluwatu's current crop of dainty and sophisticated products—achieved by highlighting the intricacy of home-grown Balinese garments and reviving traditional methods of production—have allowed Made to engage with the global business landscape on her own terms.

The ancient Uluwatu site continues to inspire the whole company, however, by symbolising its dedication to upholding local heritage. Two of Made's sisters have joined her in this growing enterprise, and they

continue to channel the unique talents of older Balinese craftspeople into creating lovely additions to the Uluwatu line. The company has also trained close to 300 staff who are dedicated to their craft, and painstakingly embroider, cut, wash, iron and pack the lace products for shipping at Uluwatu's informal factory in Tabanan, west of Denpasar. The price for maintaining such high levels of quality, however, is a low volume of production every year. This makes it difficult for the company to commit supplies to department stores, but also gives each item produced an almost exclusive quality.

The modest, down-to-earth luxury of an Uluwatu piece—whether a dress, blouse or

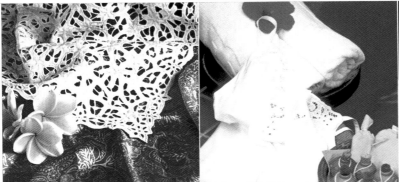

pair of trousers—is immediately visible to the knowledgeable shopper. Most items are available in three colours—black, white or cream—but to meet growing demands, Uluwatu is working on expanding the line to include other colours. The latest range also includes resort attire and casual wear perfect for use during your stay in tropical Bali. Light fabrics such as rayon, cotton and linen ensure you're kept cool.

In a culture where children develop their artistic aptitude at their parents' knees and through observing the village craftspeople, musicians and artists at work everyday,

Uluwatu is not just helping to keep a key Balinese artform alive, but also showcasing it in the international market. The bulk of each batch produced is marked for tourist retail outlets, while just under half heads overseas for wholesale dealers.

Each new wave of visitors to the island discovers that fine Uluwatu lace serves as both a unique memento that attests to Bali's rich cultural heritage, and as an intricate and impressive work of art that stands up to the stringent tests of time. This makes Uluwatu Handmade Balinese Lace so much more than just a souvenir.

THIS PAGE: When using a foot-powered machine, as Uluwatu does, the needle stays put while the craftsperson uses his or her hands to move the bamboo hoop back and forth, creating beautiful, intricate details.

OPPOSITE (FROM TOP): A lace memento from Bali makes a stunning addition to any home; beds look more inviting with embroidered white bedlinen.

FACTS

PRODUCT	lace clothing, accessories, bedlinen and table linen
FEATURES	handmade lace using traditional foot-powered machines • exclusive products
NEARBY	Sanur Beach • Pura Belanjong • Bale Banjar Batu Jimbar
CONTACT	No. 59 Jalan Danau Tondano, Sanur 80288 (head office) • telephone: +62.361.287 638 • facsimile: +62.361.287 054 • email: uluwatu@denpasar.wasantara.net.id • website: www.uluwatu.com
BRANCHES	Galleria Nusa Dua • Mall Bali Galleria, Kuta • Jalan Legian, Kuta • Jalan Bakung Sari, Kuta • Jalan Pantai, Kuta • Jalan D. Tamblingan, Sanur • Jalan Monkey Forest, Ubud

PHOTOGRAPHS COURTESY OF ULUWATU HANDMADE BALINESE LACE.

Warisan

THIS PAGE: *Warisan Gallery offers a stunning range of textiles, handmade jewellery and unique artefacts sourced from around the region.*

OPPOSITE (FROM TOP): *Antique doors like this are among the accessories you will find to furnish your home; a knack for interior styling continues to earn Warisan praise from top hotels around the world.*

In 1989 Ida Ayu Sri Cahyani and her husband launched Warisan Gallery to share their love for antique furniture and original works of art with the world. The store's initial collection of sculptures, textiles, jewellery, wood carvings and antiques, sourced from all over Bali, Java and Sumatra, took little time to earn Warisan Gallery a reputation as a haven for serious collectors and fans of traditional Indonesian style.

The present store occupies two floors with approximately 650 sq m (6,997 sq ft) of display space and a collection of antiques that are Indonesian, Chinese and Colonial Dutch in origin. Here, you'll find rattan, mahogany and bamboo furnishings, fine leather and hand-woven fabrics that form an impressive range of products. Discerning clientele will also revel in a selection of the best silk and batik creations, handmade jewellery, statues and traditional puppets that the region has to offer. Regular shows here have drawn eager customers from all corners of the globe.

Ultimately, Ida and her husband are focused on more than just selling traditional Indonesian crafts; rather they aim to share the classic elegance and relevance of their Indonesian heritage, and thus, transcend cultural barriers worldwide.

More recently, a furniture division, PT Warisan, was launched to expand their vision to cover contract furniture and lighting. Design-wise, much of the signature lines feature handcrafted quality teak and mahogany, in clean, minimalist styles. The outdoor line, in particular, is made from plantation and recycled teak, and is available in a spectrum of designs from the most contemporary look and feel to the

The collection is complemented with contemporary merchandise imported from Southeast Asia, particularly Burma, Thailand and China, and a new section which carries unique fashion accessories and household items largely designed to capture a creative fusion of East and West. The new range thus extends to eye-catching jewellery, well-made garments, luxurious leather products, and stylish home accessories including sconces, table and floor lamps, and more. Many of these are given lustrous finishes of natural oil, traditional shellac and beeswax so that their physical forms and surfaces make a distinct impression against the surroundings they eventually inhabit.

traditional. The use of genuine aged timber with these products creates an impression of hardiness and longevity, and these are themes that define the gallery's distinguished Rustic and Neo-Primitive collections.

Warisan, an environmentally-conscious manufacturer, does not use rainforest woods. Their supply of teak is obtained from around Java and Madura through the official forestry department which looks after plantation territories amounting to almost three million hectares (seven million acres). Many of the trees in these territories were planted by the Dutch colonial administration over 150 years ago and are therefore of great historical significance. Many of Warisan's products are also created from stocks of recycled teak retrieved from old buildings, bridges and other supply sources. These are often of varied and rare origin, and many have endured rough usage and extreme conditions for a century or more at least, experiencing sufficient stress to give the wood a unique look and character.

Demand for Warisan's expertise has grown enough to warrant its expansion

THIS PAGE: *The sunbed, outdoor table and bedroom set are all a part of PT Warisan's Neo-Primitive collection.*

OPPOSITE: *Resort-style private residence interiors are a growing trend.*

overseas. As a leading brand in Indonesian-produced lighting and collectible furniture, PT Warisan's more recent overseas foray has been the launch of a flagship outlet along Beverly Boulevard, in Los Angeles. This store is located in a vibrant urban centre where the preference for Asian-centric living space design has been catching on. It means the growing Warisan network will reach a new community of designers in North America who can tap into the Indonesian creative spirit, share their expertise and collaborate with Warisan in more exciting and beneficial ways.

The Warisan Lighting Collection, under the leadership of managing director Angelo Bellini, focuses on resort lighting solutions that are based on innovative illumination designs. The in-house studio puts together specific solutions based on briefs supplied by clients and creates lighting that perfectly matches the theme and mood of the venue in question. Warisan's interior consultancy has already created ideal solutions for many top establishments including the Jamison Street Hotel in Sydney and Disney's Animal Kingdom Lodge in Orlando.

Another big client, The Chedi Muscat in Oman, is an award-winning property featuring stylish furniture manufactured to Warisan's high standards.

FACTS

PRODUCTS	antique furniture • sculptures • wood carvings • textiles • jewellery • leather products • paintings • tapestries • lighting
FEATURES	plantation and recycled wood • in-house design team
NEARBY	Kafe Warisan • Pura Petitenget
CONTACT	Warisan Gallery: No. 38 Jalan Raya Kerobokan, Kerobokan, Banjar Taman, Kuta 80361 • telephone: +62.361.730 710 • facsimile: +62.361.730 047 • email: warisangallery@eksadata.com • website: www.warisan.com PT Warisan: Jalan Raya Padang, Luwih Banjar Tegal Jaya, Dalung, Kuta 80361 • telephone: +62.361.421 752 • facsimile: +62.361.421 214 • email: sales@warisan.com • website: www.warisan.com

PHOTOGRAPHS COURTESY OF WARISAN.

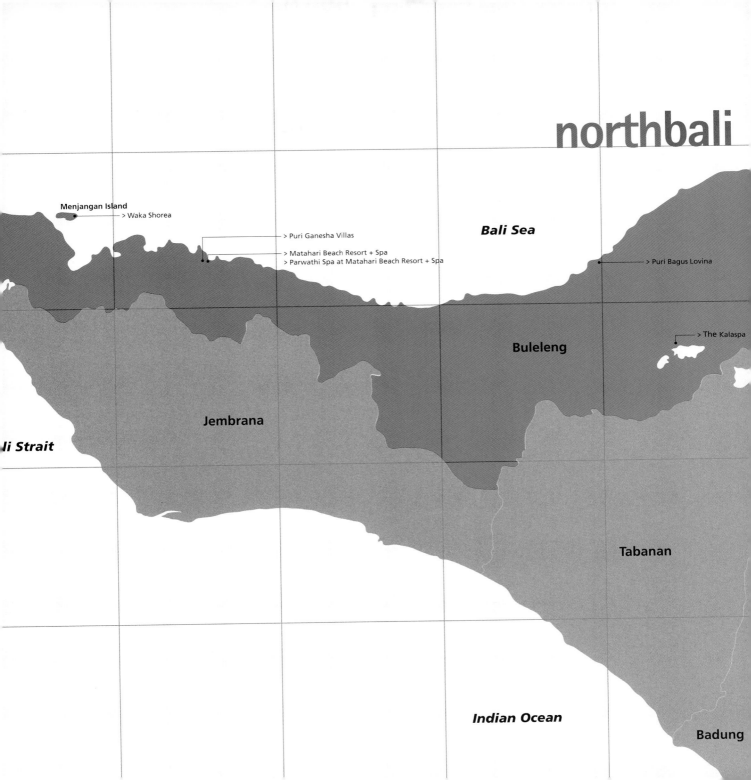

northbali

Menjangan Island
> Waka Shorea

Bali Sea

> Puri Ganesha Villas

> Matahari Beach Resort + Spa
> Parwathi Spa at Matahari Beach Resort + Spa

> Puri Bagus Lovina

> The Kalaspa

Buleleng

li Strait

Jembrana

Tabanan

Indian Ocean

Badung

the flip side of bali

Beyond the mountains that form the spine of Bali, the north feels like a parallel universe. It is still Bali, but it is a Bali with an unusual flavour. You could be on another island altogether. It is definitely different, and a lot drier than the south. Perhaps that's why those who know the island well head north for a quiet escape.

North Bali is the place to unwind, swim, snorkel, laze around, read and get away from it all. It is also ideal for a spa holiday because there are fewer distractions and the atmosphere is less intense than in the south. Buleleng Regency, which covers all of the north, has not experienced the same level of development that the south has, resulting in a much slower pace of life up this way.

On the other hand, there's more to the north than just silence and contemplation. It is Bali's supreme diving and snorkelling zone, and it has a rich history and culture all of its own. In addition to this, visitors can expect stunning scenery, deserted beaches, mysterious temples and verdant hills with views stretching down to the sea. It is definitely not a boring or featureless place. But everything does seem further away here, with a palpable distance between places.

getting there is half the fun

The parallel universe of north Bali is only a short drive away from the better known destinations of the south, and getting there is half the fun. Three main roads wind upwards over the mountains and all of them are spectacular routes for sightseeing. As the saying goes, travel is not about the destination, but the journey itself. Well, this is one journey worth taking, no matter which route you choose. Plan for plenty of pit stops and side trips during this extremely scenic drive.

One you've passed through the mountains, you will enter a visibly different setting. Parts of it look like the rugged badlands featured in cowboy movies, with parched golden bluffs towering over sage-coloured scrub. Out east, beyond Tulamben, it's a different kind of movie set altogether, with landscapes punctuated by twisted lontar

PAGE 200: The freedom fighters' monument in Singaraja.

THIS PAGE (FROM TOP): Resorts like Wake Shorea and Puri Ganesha Villas are secluded properties that offer guests a taste of Bali's quiet and scenic north.

OPPOSITE: At Tulamben, multi-hued outrigger canoes known as jukung fish the coastal waters.

trees casting spiky shadows over a vast emptiness of volcanic debris. More otherworldly still is the underwater scenery nearby, with reefs readily accessible to divers or snorkellers along the north coast—home to billions of the most bizarre creatures of the sea in every psychedelic colour combination possible.

Coming out of the water in north Bali, you will find black sand or mixed shingle beaches, some of them silent, deserted and backed by shady coconut palm groves. Beyond those groves, the coastal areas of north Bali are almost totally undeveloped, hot and dry, with occasional oases of luxury and style appearing seemingly out of the blue in the midst of those wild, open spaces. Among them are the boutique resorts of the Menjangan and Pemuteran areas towards the west, and a handful of remote hotels, dive centres, spas and small retreat resorts closer to Singaraja.

lovina: the groovy ghost town

More or less in the middle along north Bali's coast is the town of Lovina, once a booming bungalow zone populated by the backpacking youth of the 1970s and 1980s. Lovina literally boomed during that era, and cheap, funky dives popped up like mushrooms. The bubble of prosperity was short-lived, however, and Lovina was soon a town of shaggy grass roofs, and abandoned cafés and shops.

The underlying attraction of the Lovina coast is perennial, however, and includes very pleasant beaches, an accessible, shallow reef, and the ubiquitous charms of Buleleng itself—sweet fruit, sunny skies, lower prices, and informal people with hotter tempers and warmer hearts who are given to more earthy expressions of life, sexuality and the likes than their neighbours in south Bali. There's also a kind of drowsy timelessness about north Bali that can be intoxicating.

THIS PAGE (FROM TOP): The calm, quiet beaches of north Bali are a relaxing contrast to the busy beach scene in the south; Singaraja's diverse population includes descendants of early Chinese traders.

OPPOSITE: Singaraja's colourful and multi-ethnic market; a sculpture at the main roundabout of Singaraja illustrates the meaning of the city's name, which is 'lion king'.

the colonial romance of singaraja city

That sense of timelessness is felt nowhere more strongly than in the Dutch colonial town of Singaraja, the capital of Buleleng. With about 100,000 inhabitants, it is Bali's second biggest city, although not a particularly busy one, and definitely not targeted at tourists. It has a life of its own, with only a passing and very incidental interest in tourism, which is one of the reasons why it is worth visiting. It allows you to see what an Indonesian provincial city is really like.

North Bali fell to the Dutch in the middle of the 19th century, long before the rest of Bali did. The Dutch made Singaraja their administrative centre for all of Bali, although they didn't actually administer a thing anywhere else on the island until the second decade of the 20th century.

Singaraja, however, was the most vibrant city in Bali for a long time before the Dutch arrived, and before tourism brought money and diversity to the south. It was a lively commercial town with the best harbour in Bali, and had long been a popular port of call for Arab, Chinese, Bugis and Indian traders, many of whom chose to settle in Singaraja over the years. The town has distinctive Chinese and Arab quarters, and a visit to the main market on any morning gives visitors an interesting and eye-opening look at the cultural diversity of the place. It is probably the best example of the 'real, original Asia' you will find in Bali these days.

Singaraja's Dutch colonial history is apparent everywhere, with picturesque houses, shops and government buildings dating from the late 19th to the early 20th century. They show influences of the European Arts and Crafts movement, Art Nouveau and Art Deco, but with a distinct Asian colonial nuance.

These charming edifices were well constructed, and many are only now beginning to deteriorate due to a lack of maintenance. The more splendid examples virtually cry out for a foreign investor or architecture buff to come along and restore them to their former glory, or convert them into cafés or nostalgic speakeasies. But with Singaraja as sleepy as it is, this isn't likely any time soon.

an independent culture with influential eccentrics

Buleleng has its own distinct styles of architecture, carving, literature, gamelan music, dance, drama and weaving, but they are relatively unpackaged, unexposed and unexploited. This is typical of north Bali: it is not touristy or glamorous, it is just what it is and operates on its own terms only.

This uncontrived way of being is endemic at the eastern end of the coast, around Tulamben, Amed and Bunutan, in east Bali. The little hotels and bamboo bungalows that cling to this coast are a vision of hippy bliss. Most offer very little in the way of facilities or food, but the atmosphere recalls the early days of tourism in Kuta.

The vast, open coast from Tulamben, west to Singaraja, is relatively undeveloped, with miles of deserted beach ripe for a quick dip, a side trip to the Bali Aga villages just uphill, and a little exploration. There's hardly anything out here at all but a few remote resorts, some independent expatriates, and one dramatic and spiritually powerful temple called Pura Ponjok Batu, perched right over the water with sweeping

views of the sparkling sea and endless sky. Ponjok Batu is tied to the historical and mythological tales of Dang Hyang Nirartha, a Javanese super-priest who came to Bali in the 18th century on a sacred mission and became the single most formative figure in the evolution of Balinese Hinduism as it is practiced today.

Also associated with the thrilling tales of Nirartha and his mystical, magical adventures in north Bali is Pura Agung Pulaki, way out west and a long way from Ponjok Batu. Pulaki is one of the most spiritually charged places in Bali, and Hindu pilgrims, mystics and priests from all over the island come here to meditate and pray, particularly during a full moon. It is not one temple, but a complex of several, spread out along the coast, and on nearby cliffs and precipitous headlands. All of it has been lovingly modernised, employing some interesting post-modern Balinese architecture that is a potent blend of ancient history and fantasy.

harmony with nature on land and under the sea

Just west of Pulaki temple is Pemuteran town, which is a gem of a place, with delightful boutique hotels nestled between the road and peaceful waters of Pemuteran Bay.

Pemuteran's story began in the early 1990s when a Balinese tourism entrepreneur from Denpasar named Agung Prana had a vision while meditating at Pulaki temple. The Hindu god Vishnu manifested himself before Prana and delivered a mandate that he should create a resting place at Pemuteran founded on the principle of harmony between man and nature. Since Vishnu is associated with the preservation of life and water, the vision was a particularly potent one, and Prana knew what he had to do.

With the help of various western and Indonesian conservationists and Baliphiles, Prana created in Pemuteran an exclusive number of places to stay, eat and enjoy the magic of the local environment. Among these carefully crafted enterprises and programmes are a sea turtle conservation and breeding project, an exemplary and award-winning coral reef conservation project, a riding stable, several environmentally sensitive dive operations, and a whole range of programmes involving the local

THIS PAGE (FROM TOP): It is said that the gods of Pulaki temple can grant mystical powers or prosperity to devotees; mountain people of the interior still use traditional means of transport.

OPPOSITE (FROM TOP): Ponjok Batu temple is linked to the historic super-priest Nirartha; Pulaki temple is famed for the antics of its resident monkeys.

community. These programmes, and the businesses and NGOs involved in them, aim to show how tourism, the environment and the community can co-exist harmoniously and for mutual benefit. It has been an interesting experiment with many challenges, and for the most part, extremely successful. The water and beaches are clean, the reefs are in good shape, the marine life is protected and flourishing, and the community is happy.

Pemuteran is just one of the many outstanding dive locations along the north coast of Bali. Some of them are well-known, and others are just being discovered. Underwater marvels abound, with exquisite corals of all kinds and a dazzling variety of rare and beautiful creatures. Working from east to west, the most renowned sites are Bunutan, Cemeluk, Amed, Tulamben, Pemuteran and the outstanding and vast coral gardens of Menjangan Island, which is part of Bali Barat National Park and is staunchly conserved as a marine nature reserve.

As there is little rain in north Bali, the water is clearer and silt free for most of the year. The sea is also calmer than the surf-swept beaches of the south, with minimal currents. This makes it ideal for safe diving, snorkelling and swimming.

head for the hills

Eventually every visitor has to head home from north Bali but on the way back down, you'll experience the beauty of its interior, which is a fascinating mix of dramatic wilderness, picturesque villages, scenic rice terraces and plantations. The views from Buleleng's highlands back down to the Bali Sea are stunning too.

Set aside plenty of time for the trip, maybe even several days. The middle and upper elevations offer great trekking with towering rock walls, lushly forested hillsides laced with waterfalls, and mountains looming large above them all. Stretching out below are fields of grapes, sandalwood, rice and citrus fruits. Above are vast plantations of cloves and coffee. Running intermittently through it all, from the coast up into the mountain passes, are beautifully sculpted rice terraces which glow with an otherworldly green in the early morning or late afternoon light.

THIS PAGE (FROM TOP): Dramatic waterfalls are a refreshing feature of the north's terrain; traditional fishing boats line the shore at Amed in the day.
OPPOSITE: The dramatic mountain view from Puri Ganesha Villas.

...a fascinating mix of dramatic wilderness, picturesque villages, scenic rice terraces and plantations.

Matahari Beach Resort + Spa

Now and then, a visitor to Bali hears for the first time that this breathtaking locale is also famously known as the Island of the Gods, a title that pays poetic tribute to how Bali's magical allure is equal parts natural landscape and folk spiritualism. And there are few places better than Matahari Beach Resort and Spa to experience exactly what this means.

A luxurious sanctuary located in Pemuteran, north Bali, this resort—a Relais and Châteaux partner—has 16 Double Bungalows, each offering panoramic views, luxurious facilities and spacious interiors. These bungalows also bear the creative signatures of native artisans whose talents account for the handcrafted furniture found throughout the resort. These include the wooden folding door frames that mark the entrance to each bungalow, and the ornate four-poster bed found in every room, crafted from local hardwoods and featuring a golden canopy of hand-plaited raffia. The furnishings reflect a deep reverence for Bali's rich heritage, and also pay tribute to the natural wonders all around the resort, from black-sand beaches to lush, tropical growth.

In an effort to not dampen the rustic magic, the bungalows are laid out to render the more ostentatious luxuries accessible, but in ways which do not compromise the resort's natural setting. Indoor marble bathtubs, for example, are designed such that they almost blend into the surrounding tropical environment. Outdoors, in a private garden, guests will find an additional

The most frequently touted attraction at Matahari is the great snorkelling and diving available.

shower designed in a similar fashion. The resort's five-star status is indeed assurance that no guest is left wanting or feeling neglected during their stay.

The most frequently touted attraction at Matahari is the great snorkelling and diving available. The dive centre here serves as a base camp from which to explore the glorious wonders that lie in the dive sites all around. From snorkelling to diving, reef-combing to dolphin watching, the activities in and on the water here are definitely worth the three-hour journey from the airport in Denpasar to the resort.

Beginners can opt for an introductory dive class and get their full certification in the resort's pool. More experienced divers can sign up for PADI-certified open water diving

and advanced open water diving, or master scuba diver and dive master certifications. Do remember to pack your certification and log book, along with two passport-size photographs if you plan to sign up for these courses which will widen your horizons.

The waters just off the beach at Matahari are excellent for shallow shore dives. Other popular dive sites are the wreck of the USS Liberty in Tulamben, and the Menjangan Island Marine Reserve, a 40-minute boat ride from the resort. This area is part of Bali Barat National Park and is home to beautiful coral reefs, sea turtles,

THIS PAGE (FROM TOP): Enjoy a soothing massage in an outdoor pavilion; traditional Balinese structures can be found around the resort.
OPPOSITE: The bungalows feature spacious living areas both indoors and outdoors.

whale sharks, stingrays and a myriad of tropical fish. Guests at Matahari enjoy exclusive access to this dive site, with qualified instructors leading the way.

These activities will definitely work up an appetite. Before heading to dinner at Dewi Ramona, the resort's restaurant, enjoy appetisers and cocktails at Wayan Cocktail Bar. Then, take your seat at the restaurant, where the kitchen crew will whip up a tasteful juxtaposition of European styles and Indonesian flavours, best accompanied by a suitable wine and a stroll on the beach after dinner to enjoy the evening breeze. General Manager Jany-Michel Fourre is also the resort's chef de cuisine. Having worked in some of the best kitchens around Europe, his extensive experience guarantees that the menu here never falls short on flair or flavour.

Matahari ensures only the best and freshest ingredients are used by running its own fruit and vegetable farms, butchery and smoking chamber for meats. This self-suffiency extends to the resort's 100 tantalising varieties of bread and pastries prepared by their own chef. A small farm

THIS PAGE (FROM TOP): **As night falls, the resort takes on a charming glow with beautifully lit pavilions; every bungalow is surrounded by private tropical gardens.**

OPPOSITE: **Take a dip in the pool surrounded by colourful bougainvillea and hibiscus, while the scent of lilies, jasmine and frangipanis fill the air.**

ensures that ducks, geese, quails and pigeons are never in short supply for the more rare and exquisite dishes. To complement a truly homemade meal, Matahari has a wine cellar stocked with 120 selected labels to suit different menus.

Right in front of the restaurant is a stage where local Legong and Barong dancers showcase their skills. An evening of captivating entertainment like this will surely motivate you to skip water sports for a day and head out into nearby towns such as Singaraja to explore more of Balinese culture, arts and crafts. Guests can also head deeper into the countryside by joining the resort's biking tours around the local villages, or just follow the guided paths into the mountains. Take some time afterwards to experience the resort's fragrant gardens filled with colourful bougainvillea, hibiscus, lilies, jasmine and frangipani.

There is always the palatial Parwathi Spa to look forward to as well, designed in honour of the Hindu gods Shiva and Parwathi. Here, guests can indulge in relaxing treatments and therapies to heal the body, mind and spirit.

FACTS		
ROOMS	16 Double Bungalows
FOOD	Dewi Ramona Restaurant: Balinese, Indonesian and international
DRINK	Wayan Cocktail Bar • beach bistro: light snacks and beverages
FEATURES	Parwathi Spa • dive school • water sports • hiking • cultural tours • biking
BUSINESS	conference room
NEARBY	Menjangan Island • Singaraja centre
CONTACT	PO Box 194 Pemuteran, Singaraja 81155 • telephone: +62.362.92 312 • facsimile: +62.362.92 313 • email: mbr-bali@indo.net.id • website: www.matahari-beach-resort.com

PHOTOGRAPHS COURTESY OF MATAHARI BEACH RESORT AND SPA.

Puri Bagus Lovina

Lovina's first luxury resort, Puri Bagus Lovina, evokes memories of old Bali. This 20,000 sq m (23,920 sq yd) property features traditional Balinese architecture set against the beautiful backdrop of the island's north, while the Bali Sea brushes the shore on the other side of the property.

The resort's 36 spacious villas and two suites have thatched alang alang roofs, broad verandahs, satellite television and outdoor showers within the confines of a tropical garden. The suites also feature private swimming pools and open dining areas. The simple lines and clean décor reflect a contemporary outlook with tasteful applications of Balinese design elements.

Guests at this resort won't be spending too much time indoors, however, as there's just too much to do outside. The free-form swimming pool beckons constantly, but one look at the clear, blue sea ahead and you just might drop everything and run with exuberance towards the 200-m (219-yd) stretch of beach that fronts the hotel.

Make the most of your time in the water by engaging in activites like sailing, snorkelling, scuba diving and windsurfing. This region is actually home to lovely

THIS PAGE (FROM TOP): Every villa has an outdoor shower in a private walled garden; the spacious villas offer a comfortable place to rest after a day spent enjoying the resort's many outdoor activities.
OPPOSITE: Choose between a leisurely swim in the pool or a refreshing dip in the Bali Sea.

coral formations which will provide hours of delightful exploration. If you're really lucky, you might even spot dolphins frolicking in the vicinity, especially in the early morning. Guests can also embark on a breakfast or dinner cruise along the scenic coasts of Singaraja and Lovina respectively.

Should you feel the need for a little pampering or relaxation, Jaya Spa offers services ranging from massages to body scrubs, reflexology and various beauty treatments, all of which can be enjoyed in an open-air setting right on the beach.

Outside the resort, there is even more to see. In fact, the transfer from the airport in south Bali to the resort will give you a preview of what to expect, from culturally-rich sights, to expansive beaches, verdant rice fields and much more.

Indeed, there are a host of venues to visit, all just a stone's throw from the resort. Banjar Village is a 30-minute drive away and is home to a Buddhist temple and a popular hot springs site. Similarly, the temples at Medue Karang and Sangsit Village, and the Gitgit waterfall, are also

conveniently located. Pura Jagatnatha, the biggest temple in this area, is worth a visit, as is Taman Ayun, another of Bali's more popular temples. Known for its distinctive moat and walkways, an afternoon spent exploring this temple will surely open your eyes to the beauty of Balinese architecture.

Some of the more notable attractions, though, lie just further out. These include Bali Handara Golf Course, Ulun Danu Temple on Lake Beratan, and the Botanical Gardens in nearby Bedugul. Bird-watchers will no doubt flock to Bali Barat National Park to

THIS PAGE (FROM TOP): **Views of the sea can be enjoyed from almost every villa; cocktails at sunset in a cosy pavilion add a little romance to your beach holiday.**

OPPOSITE (FROM TOP): **The resort can organise private dinners on the beach; high, thatched roofs and spacious interiors create an open and airy feel.**

get up close and personal with many indigenous species of birds, including the Bali Starling, while underwater enthusiasts might prefer a trip to Menjangan Island. Not to be missed is a day trip to Mount Batur to view its 14-km- (nine-mile-) wide crater which features a crescent-shaped mountain lake and a new volcanic cone. There is also the local market at Candi Kuning, a favourite with those who enjoy the sights, sounds and smells of such places.

Bookworms should not feel excluded from these activities and distractions. There's reassuring refuge to be found in the resort's dedicated reading room, which houses a satisfying selection of travelogues and pictorial books about native arts and cultures. Beyond the resort, there are also fascinating historical documents and manuscripts available for scrutiny at the Gedung Kerlya Museum, located in nearby Singaraja. These are commonly referred to as the Lontar Manuscripts, on account of them having been etched onto the leaves of the lontar palm. The collection includes old Javanese, Balinese and other Indonesian scripts on a range of subjects including religion, medicine and mythology. A lesser known fact is that the weaving factory behind the resort's library produces beautiful silk and cotton fabrics, and is worth a visit.

When all your explorations are done for the day, it's time to satisfy your palate

with a meal at the resort's restaurant. Housed in a pavilion, the restaurant features charming views of the gardens and the sea. Guests can tuck into sumptuous local and international fare including favourites such as Grilled Tiger Prawns, Oceana La Darma (Balinese clams with a cream sauce), Soto Ayam (clear chicken soup with a boiled egg and glass noodles), Ikan Bakar (a whole fish grilled over lava stones and served with vegetables and ceremonial Balinese yellow rice) and a whole lot more.

With so much to see and do, Puri Bagus Lovina is effectively your gateway to Bali's north. Whether you choose to stay within the property for the duration of your trip, or explore the surrounding areas, you will never find yourself bored here.

FACTS		
ROOMS	36 villas • 2 suites	
FOOD	Balinese and international	
DRINK	bar	
FEATURES	pool • spa • beach • water sports • cruises	
BUSINESS	library • meeting room	
NEARBY	hot springs • coral formations • temples • Mount Batur • Menjangan Island	
CONTACT	Jalan Raya Seririt Singaraja, Desa Pemaron, PO Box 225, Lovina, Singaraja 81151 • telephone: +62.362.214 30 • facsimile: +62.362.226 27 • email: puribaguslovina@bagus-discovery.com • website: www.bagus-discovery.com	

PHOTOGRAPHS COURTESY OF PURI BAGUS LOVINA.

Puri Ganesha Villas

THIS PAGE: *Puri Ganesha offers many comfortable spots where guests can relax and unwind, both indoors and outdoors.*

OPPOSITE: *The open terraces have been designed to provide a grand view of the surroundings.*

If you are looking for a place in the sun, set against an unspoilt backdrop of tropical beauty, then the fact that Puri Ganesha Villas has been called one of travel's best-kept secrets will definitely make you sit up and take notice.

Puri Ganesha, set in the fishing village of Pemuteran, near Bali Barat National Park, has about 400 m (437 yd) of inviting beachfront. What appears on first approach as a modest string of houses soon emerges into view as a collection of tasteful and inviting villas. Most guests are immediately awed by this lush and sprawling space which conveys both grandeur and exoticism through simple touches like antique carved doors and isolated beachside pavilions.

The resort's four two-storey villas have different themes, each appearing distinct yet aesthetically complementary. Villa Senyum takes its cue from the pretty bougainvillea and is dressed up in lively shades of pink, while Villa Sepi expresses a slightly more contemplative tone and is layered with handmade fabrics in blue, white and hues of chocolate brown. These villas have one master bedroom and a second room with twin beds. Villa Senang, a three-bedroom villa, is an energetic celebration of purple, terracotta and yellow. Finally, there is Villa

Santai, the honeymoon villa with one master bedroom. It makes an elegant impression with its interplay of black and white, and gold and silver contrasts. Each villa features a private swimming pool and garden, along with a beachfront antique rice barn for relaxation, and an open-air poolside pavilion where guests can enjoy their daily meals. The villas also come with two personal staff and the services of a butler.

Indeed, there is little else to do in a place like this but revel in the solitude and scenic setting. Not that there would be much time to squander between stints of lazing in the sun, floating around the pool, unwinding under the masterly hands of the massage therapists, and sampling the culinary creations from the impressive kitchen.

The restaurant here serves Balinese and international dishes prepared with organic produce obtained from suppliers residing in the nearby mountains, and fresh fish, chicken and seafood from the local markets. Guests may choose to have their meals in the communal setting of the restaurant, or in their villa. Either way, mealtimes are one of the highlights of the day here.

Worthy of special mention among the many notable dishes are the Lemon Grass Tuna cooked with roast garlic and served with mashed potatoes and carrots, and the Prawns, Swordfish and Spices in Banana

Leaf, accompanied by a serving of stir-fried local vegetables. The dinner menu focuses on health and energy, and varies from one evening to the next. From salads to pasta and Oriental classics, the dinner table has seen almost every type of food, except red meat. Everything served here is also devoid of artificial additives in order to facilitate a complete detoxifying diet during your stay.

Ecological concerns have inspired a no-plastic policy on the resort's grounds, effectively banning the presence of plastic drinking containers and bottles. The drinking water provided has been sourced from a

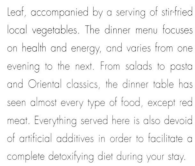

THIS PAGE (FROM TOP): **Enjoy views of the Bali Sea from your own beachfront pavilion; every villa has its own dining area where guests can enjoy a healthy and organic meal.**

OPPOSITE: **Private pools are another luxury afforded by Puri Ganesha.**

local spring found in Sanggalngit, which is a famous source of spring water in Bali.

As for activities, there is a boat for charter if guests would like to head out in search of dolphins or breathtaking sunsets. Those keen to check out the lay of the land can sign up for one of the educational spice tours and treks. A more exciting approach would be to join the horseback riding tours, led by an experienced trainer, along the beach and into the nearby village.

By far the most remarkable attraction of Puri Ganesha, however, is its atmosphere of love and romance. This goes beyond the wedding and honeymoon packages which are a staple of many resorts up and down the coast. Puri Ganesha has been nothing short of a legendary labour of love for owner Diana von Cranach who journeyed to this island in the wake of a past marriage and ended up not only establishing a luxury

destination but also finding new love. Today, her husband Gusti plays proud co-proprietor, and mixes one refreshing cocktail after another for similarly happy guests.

The wedding services provided here come complete with traditional formalities and spiritual blessings, and favour a green and white theme that unifies the entire event from the décor right down to the wedding feast. For those celebrating anniversaries with their children in tow, it will be a great relief to learn that the staff at Puri Ganesha are most sincere about baby-sitting and make engaging and instructive playmates.

Make the most of a visit to Bali's unspoiled northwest coast by staying at Puri Ganesha Villas. This cosy resort offers the comfort, intimacy and personal service you might find at a country homestay, but with all the luxury of a larger hotel, making it popular with couples and small families.

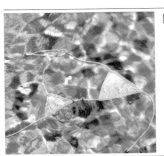

FACTS

ROOMS	4 villas
FOOD	Balinese and international • no red meat
DRINK	cocktails at the restaurant
FEATURES	private pools • beach • cooking classes • massages
BUSINESS	IDD telephone
NEARBY	Menjangan Island • horseback riding • spice farms
CONTACT	Pantai Pemuteran, Gerokgak, Singaraja 81155 • telephone: +62.362.947 66 • facsimile: +62.362.934 33 • email: pganesha@indosat.net.id • website: www.puriganesha.com

PHOTOGRAPHS COURTESY OF PURI GANESHA VILLAS.

Waka Shorea

Hidden away on Menjangan Island in Bali's northwest, just over three hours away from the airport, Waka Shorea is the sole resort allowed within territory belonging to Bali Barat National Park. It takes pride in being an environmental sanctuary, off the beaten track and full of activities for nature-lovers and those who love water sports in particular. Not only does this unobtrusive property not compromise the area's status as a national ecological reserve, it allows its guests to relish in an environment designed to embrace nature's beauty.

This cosy retreat has 14 bungalows and two villas. Everything inside reflects the rich textures and colours of the surrounding nature park: slate, smooth, unpainted wood, homespun fabrics and the occasional metalwork artefact. If the décor generally strikes you as slightly more dramatic and jungle-like than expected, it is because the resort's inspiration was Kenya's Treetops Hotel. As a result, the villas and dining and massage pavilions were designed to extend over the trees, leaving guests with breathtaking views of the forest and the inviting sea just beyond.

When mealtime arrives, guests will find they are not restricted to dining at the restaurant. In fact, a number of options are available including candlelit dinners on the

THIS PAGE (FROM TOP): *Water sports enthusiasts will treasure their experiences at Waka Shorea; the resort's architecture is designed to complement the natural environment.*

OPPOSITE: *Rooms are furnished simply but with all the expected comforts.*

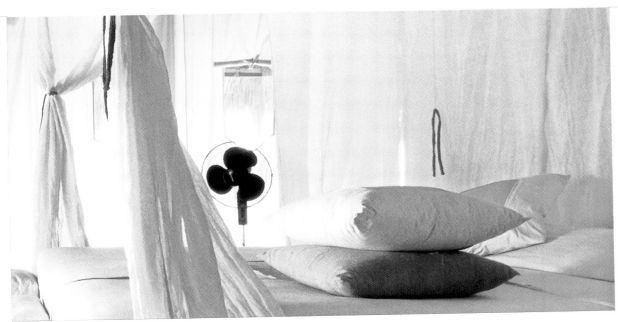

jetty, by the pool or on the beach. You can even enjoy a gourmet picnic on a secluded beach to enjoy a little romance.

Water sports enthusiasts will surely fill their days with sailing, kayaking, scuba diving, snorkelling and canoeing, or just swimming leisurely in the pool. This area is well-known for providing some of Bali's best diving, so be sure to come prepared with all the appropriate dive certifications.

Back on solid ground, guests can set off on a number of nature treks to seek out native deer and the elusive silver or black leaf monkey. Alternatively, enjoy a quiet day spent bird-watching and you could find yourself rewarded with a glimpse of the Bali Starling, a small white bird with a blue streak around its eyes, found only in Bali.

A back-to-nature experience is truly what Waka Shorea offers. But even if nature treks and water sports are not your cup of tea, the resort is still a great choice if you're hoping to escape from the crowds and the pressures of city life.

FACTS		
	ROOMS	14 bungalows • 2 villas
	FOOD	restaurant: Balinese, Indonesian and Western • barbecue area
	DRINK	bar
	FEATURES	pool • spa • trekking• water sports
	NEARBY	Bali Barat National Park • Lovina
	CONTACT	Labuan Lalang, Menjangan Island 81155 • telephone: +62.362.946 66 • facsimile: +62.362.944 99 • email: wakashorea@wakaexperience.com • website: www.wakaexperience.com

PHOTOGRAPHS COURTESY OF WAKA SHOREA.

The Kalaspa

Far off in the cool, mountainous 'lake district' of Bali, near the town of Bedugul, lies The Kalaspa, a resort designed to embrace guests of all ages, with diverging interests and needs. It lies along the calm shores of Lake Beratan, but is also close to the less frequented Lake Buyan and Lake Tamblingan. Located 1,200 m (3,937 ft) above sea level, this is an area where temperatures can sink as low as -22°C (-7.6°F) when night falls, invigorating guests with the chilly mountain air.

The Kalaspa is the ideal venue for a memorable holiday. Its accommodation consists of two Family Villas and six Private Villas, all done up in a traditional Balinese style that is cosy and alluring. Every villa commands a priceless view of both the

THIS PAGE: The majestic bedrooms look out over a rugged mountainous landscape.

OPPOSITE: Enjoy a traditional massage in the expert hands of The Kalaspa's therapists.

lake and the valley. The Family Villas are two-storey structures with a bedroom for the children downstairs, along with a dining room, and a second bedroom for the parents upstairs. The Private Villas are perfect for couples, who are assured of all the quality time they need. These secluded villas feature private balconies that look out over the northern shore, and on good days, guests might even catch a glimpse of the Bali Sea glistening in the horizon.

When it comes to dining, The Kalaspa is a stand-out choice, and regularly holds food appreciation dinners. Pakis Wine and Dine is the resort's signature restaurant and fusion cuisine is its focus. The chefs here have created a menu that uses a mix of local and imported ingredients, including vegetables cultivated on the resort's grounds. Come dinner time, the warm and romantic ambience of the restaurant allows guests to contemplate the stars above while enjoying the intermingling of flavours outlined by the use of spices, freshwater fish and highland vegetables, accentuated with a fragrant cup of Balinese coffee or Javanese black tea. Perennial favourites include the Spicy Vegetables and Chicken Bundles, Aromatic Noodle Soup with Striploin, and the Snapper Fillet Steamed in Turmeric Leaves, served with rice steamed in coconut milk. End the meal on a refreshing note with a

serving of Passion Fruit with Pineapple Juice and Pisang Ambon Liqueur. The adaptive kitchen can also accommodate requests from guests with regards to varying tastes, preparation styles or diets.

If the dining room and its formal setting is not what you're looking for, ask for a picnic basket instead and enjoy a meal outdoors while taking in the surroundings.

...you'll be left to appreciate the natural serenity of this lakeside retreat.

THIS PAGE: Pack a picnic and dine high above the lake in complete privacy.
OPPOSITE: A candlelit canopy under the trees sets the scene for yet another memorable meal.

Guests can also arrange for Balinese cooking classes with the chefs. This highly interactive session involves shopping for ingredients at the local market, picking fresh produce from the resort's grounds, preparing the meal, of course, and also setting the table properly and presenting your dishes.

As a comprehensive spa destination, The Kalaspa offers an extensive range of spa therapies including aromatherapy, herbal and bath therapies and meditative yoga. The Kalaspa's Ayurvedic approach essentially brings together your body and mind in a holistic engagement through meditation, herbal remedies and exercises. The therapists routinely pose a discreet questionnaire on guests' diets, their health problems and physical ailments before starting any treatment, in order to customise the programme. The Spa Centre itself is fully equipped with a jacuzzi, aromatic sauna, lounge, massage room, meditation hall and a well-stocked boutique.

Romance and sensual energy are dominant themes at The Kalaspa, especially for those on their honeymoon. The highlight is a holistic programme that takes nothing for granted, treating couples to an aphrodisiac-themed menu and sensual massages, all aimed at adding that extra spark to your honeymoon. Ladies will also be treated to the exclusive and traditional Secret of Royal Javanese Brides package, which promises to leave you feeling like a queen.

The globe-trotting business executive, on the other hand, will find outstanding value in the Executive Hideaway programme, which structures a series of therapies and physical exertions around a golf sojourn, and includes three days at a private villa. The fee covers a round of golf at the scenic 18-hole golf course nearby, luxurious spa

treatments, gourmet spa cuisine, outbound trips and a course in yoga or meditation.

The adventurous at heart will indeed have many sights to seek out and much terrain to conquer. Exploring nature is the primary activity here, with fishing, canoeing and trekking among the most popular options. In nearby Bedugul, guests can embark on cultural tours, with visits to numerous museums, markets and temples, including Pura Ulun Danu, a famous temple dedicated to the goddess of prosperity, Dewi Sri. There's also the Bali Berry Farm to explore—the sole strawberry farm near the resort. A little further out is the Bali Botanical Garden and Candi Kuning Fruit Market where you can get your hands on a colourful array of tropical fruit.

Just under three hours from the airport in the south, The Kalaspa offers guests a different side of Bali. Up in the mountains, the sand and the surf will seem miles away, and you'll be left to appreciate the natural serenity of this lakeside retreat.

FACTS		
	ROOMS	2 Family Villas • 6 Private Villas
	FOOD	Pakis Wine and Dine: fusion • Spa Lounge: spa and vegetarian
	DRINK	mini-bar
	FEATURES	lake • spa • trekking • fishing • canoeing
	NEARBY	Pura Ulun Danu • Bali Berry Farm • Bali Botanical Garden • Candi Kuning Fruit Market
	CONTACT	Banjar Asahpanji, Desa Wanagiri, Kecamatan Sukasada, Kabupatan Buleleng 81161 • telephone: +62.361.419 606 • facsimile: +62.361.413 060 • email: sales@kalaspa.com • website: www.kalaspa.com

PHOTOGRAPHS COURTESY OF THE KALASPA.

Parwathi Spa at Matahari Beach Resort + Spa

THIS PAGE: *Parwathi Spa was designed to resemble an ancient royal palace, with ornate carved stone entrances welcoming guests.*

OPPOSITE: *Water features and tropical flowers play their part to evoke a feeling of calm.*

Far from being yet another clinical health outift for those who wish to escape the harsh knocks of urban living, the luxurious Parwathi Spa at Matahari Beach Resort and Spa is a retreat that makes a sincere effort to pamper visitors with its range of treatments.

The healing experience actually begins during the journey from the airport in Bali's

south to the island's north coast, about three hours away. The further you get from Bali's tourist belt, the greener and more lush the landscape becomes, until the sea appears suddenly ahead of you. The natural rhythms of this tropical island provide a soothing and hypnotic backdrop against which your senses will be reinvigorated.

Deep within Parwathi Spa is an arresting arrangement of water fountains and abundant greenery, designed with a refined and almost palatial touch. This sensory seduction extends to the realm of smell too, as the heady scents of frangipani and lotus drift in from the gardens on a gentle sea breeze. With such a focus on

...an arresting arrangement of water fountains and abundant greenery...

setting the scene for complete healing, guests cannot help but succumb to feelings of complete bliss following a therapeutic regime at the hands of the experts here.

Parwathi Spa has earned its standing within the regional wellness scene on account of the sthira and sukha massages that it offers. The former can be enjoyed as part of a deluxe package that begins with a relaxing footbath, followed by a body scrub and body mask. The sthira massage is next: it is a revitalising treatment designed to alleviate stress and mental fatigue by releasing blocked energy from your muscles and connective tissues. This energy is then redirected throughout the body to create balance. Hydrotherapy and a relaxing tea ceremony end this treatment.

The sukha massage is available in a similar package. This treatment, however, focuses on the repetitive application of extended, rhythmic massage strokes that both stimulate and comfort energy points in the body, ultimately calming the mind and balancing the flow of life energies.

For those who can't bear to part with the sun, the sand and the sea for even an hour, there's the inviting option of a traditional Balinese massage, enjoyed in a private beachfront pavilion.

FACTS

TREATMENTS	massages • body wraps, scrubs and masks • facials • manicures and pedicures • hair repair
FOOD	Dewi Ramona Restaurant: Balinese, Indonesian and international
DRINK	Wayan Cocktail Bar • beach bistro: light snacks and beverages
FEATURES	shtira and sukha massages • dive school • water sports • hiking • cultural tours
NEARBY	Menjangan Island • Singaraja
CONTACT	PO Box 194 Pemuteran, Singaraja 81155 • telephone: +62.362.92 312 • facsimile: +62.362.92 313 • email: mbr-bali@indo.net.id • website: www.matahari-beach-resort.com

PHOTOGRAPHS COURTESY OF PARWATHI SPA AT MATAHARI BEACH RESORT AND SPA.

index

picturecredits

The publisher would like to thank the following for permission to reproduce their photographs:

Alila Manggis 15

Alila Ubud front cover: infinity-edged pool, 32 (top)

Tim Auger back cover: Bali Museum and stone carving, 114 (below), 115 (below)

The Avatara front cover: greenery, sculpture and panelling

Bagus Jati front cover: floral details, front flap: pool, 16, 17, 32 (below)

Choo Lip Sin 114 (top)

John Cooke back cover: ducks, 13 (below), 21 (top), 23 (top), 29 (below)

Haveli 113 (below), 119 (below)

Henna Spa and Richard Watson back flap: treatment and spa details, 120 (top)

Hotel Tugu Bali 110, 112 (below)

Hu'u Bar 117

Ibah Luxury Villas back flap: poolside

Kirana Spa 33

Koes Karnadi 12, 26 (top), 27, 200, 204, 205, 206 (below), 207 (top), 208 (top)

Ku Dè Ta and Christopher Leggett 116 (below), 118

Maya Ubud Resort and Spa 6, 8-9

The Oberoi, Bali 116 (top), 120 (below), 121

Jim Parks back cover: Mount Batur and Bali Aga villager, 24, 206 (top), 207 (below)

Puri Ganesha Villas 5 (top), 203 (below), 209

Guido Alberto Rossi 14

Spa at Ibah Luxury Villas front flap: courtyard

Tony Tilford back cover: cut rice and south Bali surf, 28, 31, 108, 111, 112 (top)

Uluwatu Handmade Balinese Lace 119 (top)

Uma Ubud front cover: chairs, doorway and stone sculpture

Villa Balquisse 2, 4

Waka di Ume front cover: tea served on wooden table, 25 (top)

Waka Shorea front flap: view from balcony over the trees, 203 (top)

Richard Watson back cover: rice terraces, 13 (top), 18, 20, 21 (below), 22, 23 (below), 25 (below), 26 (below), 30 (top and right), 113 (top), 115 (top), 202, 208 (below)

directory

Alila Manggis
Buitan, Manggis, Karangasem 80871
telephone : +62.363.410 11
facsimile : +62.363.410 15
manggis@alilahotels.com
www.alilahotels.com

Alila Ubud
Desa Melinggih Kelod, Payangan,
Ubud 80572
telephone : +62.361.975 963
facsimile : +62.361.975 968
ubud@alilahotels.com
www.alilahotels.com

Ary's Warung
Jalan Raya Ubud, Ubud 80571
telephone : +62.361.975 053
facsimile : +62.361.978 359
aryswarung@dekco.com
www.dekco.com

The Avatara
Banjar Nyanyi, Desa Beraban,
Tabanan 82121
telephone +62.361.754 344
facsimile +62.361.752 744
info@theavatara.com
www.theavatara.com

Bagus Jati
Desa Sebatu, Kecamatan Tegallalang,
PO Box 4, Ubud 80572
telephone : +62.361.978 885
facsimile : +62.361.974 666
info@bagusjati.com
www.bagusjati.com

Bali Niksoma
Jalan Padma Utara, Legian Kaja,
Legian 80361
telephone : +62.361.751 946
facsimile : +62.361.753 587
baliniksoma@indosat.net.id
www.baliniksoma.com

The Chedi Club at Tanah Gajah
Jalan Goa Gajah, Tengkulak Kaja,
Ubud 80571
telephone : +62.361.975 685
facsimile : +62.361.975 686
resort@thechediclububud.com
www.ghmhotels.com

The Club at The Legian
Jalan Laksmana, Seminyak Beach 80361
telephone : +62.361.730 622
facsimile : +62.361.730 623
legian@ghmhotels.com
www.ghmhotels.com

Haveli
Nos. 15 and 38 Jalan Basangkasa,
Seminyak 80361
telephone : +62.361.737 160
facsimile : +62.361.724 497
haveli@equinoxtrading.com
www.equinoxtrading.com

Henna Spa at Villa Balquisse
Jalan Uluwatu 18X, Jimbaran 80361
telephone : +62.361.701 695
facsimile : +62.361.701 695
info@balquisse.com
www.balquisse.com

Hotel Tugu Bali
Jalan Pantai Batu Bolong, Canggu 80361
telephone : +62.361.731 701
facsimile : +62.361.731 704
bali@tuguhotels.com
www.tuguhotels.com

Hu'u Bar
No. 1 Gang Gagak, Jalan Petitenget,
Kerobokan, Kuta 80361
telephone : +62.361.736 443
facsimile : +62.361.736 573
huubali@indo.net.id
www.huubali.com

Ibah Luxury Villas
Puri Tjampuhan, Ubud 80571
telephone : +62.361.974 466
facsimile : +62.361.974 467
ibah@dps.centrin.net.id
www.ibahbali.com

The Istana
Jalan Labuan Sait, Pantai Sulubar,
Uluwatu 80361
telephone : +62.361.730 668
facsimile : +62.361.736 566
agents@balihomes.com
www.theistana.com

Jenggala Keramik Bali
Jalan Uluwatu II, Jimbaran 80361
telephone : +62.361.703 311
facsimile : +62.361.703 312
info@jenggala-bali.com
www.jenggala-bali.com

Kafe Warisan
No. 38 Jalan Raya Kerobokan,
Banjar Taman, Kuta 80361
telephone : +62.361.731 175
facsimile : +62.361.732 762
info@kafewarisan.com
www.kafewarisan.com

The Kalaspa
Banjar Asahpanji, Desa Wanagiri,
Kecamatan Sukasada,
Kabupatan Buleleng 81161
telephone : +62.361.419 606
facsimile : +62.361.413 060
sales@kalaspa.com
www.kalaspa.com

Kedai
Jalan Raya Candidasa, Candidasa,
Karangasem 80851
telephone : +62.363.420 20
facsimile : +62.361.420 18
kedai@dekco.com
www.dekco.com

Khaima Restaurant
Jalan Laksmana, Seminyak 80361
telephone : +62.361.742 3925
facsimile : +62.361.738 627
khaima@equinoxtrading.com
www.equinoxtrading.com

Kirana Spa
Desa Kedewatan, Ubud 80571
telephone : +62.361.976 333
facsimile : +62.361.974 888
info-english@kiranaspa.com
www.kiranaspa.com

Komaneka Resort
Jalan Monkey Forest, Ubud 80571
telephone : +62.361.976 090
facsimile : +62.361.977 140
sales@komaneka.com
www.komaneka.com

Komaneka Tanggayuda
Banjar Tanggayuda, Kedewatan, Ubud 80571
telephone : +62.361.978 123
facsimile : +62.361.973 084
sales@komaneka.com
www.komaneka.com

Ku Dé Ta
No. 9 Jalan Laksmana, Seminyak Beach 80361
telephone : +62.361.736 969
facsimile : +62.361.736 767
info@kudeta.net
www.kudeta.net

Lamak Restaurant and Bar
Jalan Monkey Forest, Ubud 80571
telephone : +62.361.974 668
facsimile : +62.361.973 482
ptlamak@indosat.net.id
www.lamakbali.com

The Legian
Jalan Laksmana, Seminyak Beach 80361
telephone : +62.361.730 622
facsimile : +62.361.730 623
legian@ghmhotels.com
www.ghmhotels.com

Matahari Beach Resort and Spa
PO Box 194 Pemuteran, Singaraja 81155
telephone : +62.362.92 312
facsimile : +62.362.92 313
mbr-bali@indo.net.id
www.matahari-beach-resort.com

Maya Ubud Resort and Spa
Jalan Gunung Sari, Peliatan, Ubud 80571
telephone : +62.361.977 888
facsimile : +62.361.977 555
info@mayaubud.com
www.mayaubud.com

Natura Resort and Spa
Banjar Laplapan, Ubud 80571
telephone : +62.361.978 666
facsimile : +62.361.978 222
natura@indosat.net.id
www.bali-natura.com

The Oberoi, Bali
Jalan Laksmana, Seminyak Beach 80361
telephone : +62.361.730 361
facsimile : +62.361.730 791
reservations@theoberoi-bali.com
www.oberoihotels.com

Parwathi Spa at Matahari Beach Resort
PO Box 194 Pemuteran, Singaraja 81155
telephone : +62.362.92 312
facsimile : +62.362.92 313
mbr-bali@indo.net.id
www.matahari-beach-resort.com

Pita Maha Resort and Spa
Jalan Sanggingan, PO Box 198, Ubud 80571
telephone : +62.361.974 330
facsimile : +62.361.974 329
pitamaha@indosat.net.id
www.pitamaha-bali.com

Puri Bagus Lovina
Jalan Raya Seririt Singaraja, Desa Pemaron,
PO Box 225, Lovina, Singaraja 81151
telephone : +62.362.214 30
facsimile : +62.362.226 27
puribaguslovina@bagus-discovery.com
www.bagus-discovery.com

Puri Ganesha Villas
Pantai Pemuteran, Gerokgak,
Singaraja 81155
telephone : +62.362.947 66
facsimile : +62.362.934 33
pganesha@indosat.net.id
www.puriganesha.com

Puri Wulandari
Desa Kedewatan, Ubud 80571
telephone : +62.361.980 252
facsimile : +62.361.980 253
reservation@puriwulandari.net
www.puriwulandari.net

Sienna Villas
No.5 Gang Keraton, Jalan Raya Seminyak,
Seminyak 80361
telephone : +62.361.734 698
facsimile : +62.361.732 585
info@sienna-villas.com
www.sienna-villas.com

Spa at Ibah Luxury Villas
Tjampuhan, Ubud 80571
telephone : +62.361.974 466
facsimile : +62.361.974 467
ibah@dps.centrin.net.id
www.ibahbali.com

Taman Bebek
Sayan, Ubud 80571
telephone : +62.361.975 385
facsimile : +62.361.976 532
info@tamanbebek.com
www.tamanbebek.com

Tirtha Uluwatu
Jalan Raya Uluwatu, Banjar Karang Boma,
Uluwatu 80361
telephone : +62.361.772 255
facsimile : +62.361.777 252
wedding-coordinator@tirthabali.com
www.tirtha.com

Toko Antique
Jalan Raya Ubud,
Ubud 80571
telephone : +62.361.975 979
facsimile : +62.361.978 359
tokoantique@dekco.com
www.dekco.com

Toko East
Jalan Raya Ubud,
Ubud 80571
telephone : +62.361.978 306
facsimile : +62.361.978 359
tokoeast@dekco.com

Treasures
Jalan Raya Ubud,
Ubud 80571
telephone : +62.361.976 697
facsimile : +62.361.978 359
treasures@dekco.com
treasures.dekco.com

Uluwatu Handmade Balinese Lace
No. 59 Jalan Danau Tondano,
Sanur 80288
(head office)
telephone : +62.361.287 638
facsimile : +62.361.287 054
uluwatu@denpasar.wasantara.net.id
www.uluwatu.com

Uma Ubud
Jalan Raya Sanggingan, Banjar Lungsiakan,
Kedewatan, Ubud 80571
telephone : +62.361.972 448
facsimile : +62.361.972 449
res.ubud@uma.como.bz
uma.como.bz

Villa Balquisse
Jalan Uluwatu 18X, Jimbaran 80361
telephone : +62.361.701 695
facsimile : +62.361.701 695
info@balquisse.com
www.balquisse.com

The Villas Bali Hotel and Spa
Jalan Kunti 118 X, Seminyak 80361
telephone : +62.361.730 840
facsimile : +62.361.733 751
bookings@thevillas.net
www.thevillas.net

Waka di Ume
Jalan Sueta, Ubud 80571
telephone : +62.361.973 178
facsimile : +62.361.973 179
wakadiume@wakaexperience.com
www.wakaexperience.com

Waka Gangga
Banjar Yeh Gangga, Desa Sudimara,
Tabanan 82123
telephone : +62.361.416 256
facsimile : +62.361.416 353
wakagangga@wakaexperience.com
www.wakaexperience.com

Waka Namya
Penestanan Street, Ubud 80571
telephone : +62.361.975 719
facsimile : +62.361.975 719
wakanamya@wakaexperience.com
www.wakaexperience.com

Waka Shorea
Labuan Lalang, Menjangan Island 81155
telephone : +62.362.946 66
facsimile : +62.362.944 99
wakashorea@wakaexperience.com
www.wakaexperience.com

Warisan Gallery
No. 38 Jalan Raya Kerobokan,
Banjar Taman, Kuta 80361
telephone : +62.361.730 710
facsimile : +62.361.730 047
warisangallery@eksadata.com
www.warisan.com

PT Warisan
Jalan Raya Padang, Luwih Banjar Tegal Jaya,
Dalung, Kuta 80361
telephone : +62.361.421 752
facsimile : +62.361.421 214
sales@warisan.com
www.warisan.com